LOOKING FOR LINCOLN IN ILLINOIS

LOOKING FOR LINCOLN IN ILLINOIS

LINCOLN AND MORMON COUNTRY

Bryon C. Andreasen

Southern Illinois University Press
Carbondale

Copyright © 2015 by the Illinois Historic Preservation Agency
Foreword copyright © 2015 by the Board of Trustees,
Southern Illinois University
Portions of the text originally appeared on wayside storyboards in
several western Illinois counties within the Abraham Lincoln
National Heritage Area, produced under the direction of the
Looking for Lincoln Heritage Coalition.
Printed in the United States of America

18 17 16 15   4 3 2 1

Cover illustrations (clockwise from top): photo of Abraham
Lincoln, by William Judkins Thomson, Monmouth, Illinois,
October 11, 1858; statue of Lincoln, by Avard Fairbank, at New
Salem State Historic Site (image cropped); Mormon temple at
Nauvoo, Illinois (image cropped); Thomas and Emily Lincoln
beside Lincoln banner that now hangs in Springfield's Old State
Capitol; Tinsley Building, Springfield (image cropped); bronze
relief of Quincy's Lincoln-Douglas debate, by Lorado Taft
(image cropped). All images courtesy of the Abraham Lincoln
Presidential Library and the Illinois Historic Preservation Agency.

Library of Congress Cataloging-in-Publication Data
Andreasen, Bryon C.
Looking for Lincoln in Illinois : Lincoln and Mormon country /
Bryon C. Andreasen.
pages cm
Includes bibliographical references and index.
ISBN 978-0-8093-3384-4 (pbk. : alk. paper)
ISBN 0-8093-3384-8 (pbk. : alk. paper)
ISBN 978-0-8093-3385-1 (e-book)
ISBN 0-8093-3385-6 (e-book)
1. Lincoln, Abraham, 1809–1865—Homes and haunts—Illinois—
Anecdotes. 2. Lincoln, Abraham, 1809–1865—Friends and
associates—Anecdotes. 3. Mormons—Illinois—History—
19th century—Anecdotes. 4. Historic sites—Illinois—
Guidebooks. 5. Illinois—Guidebooks. I. Title.
E457.35.A58 2015
977.3—dc23   2015010580

The paper used in this publication meets the minimum requirements
of American National Standard for Information Sciences—
Permanence of Paper for Printed Library Materials,
ANSI Z39.48-1992. ♾

For John Hoffman—mentor, friend,
and keeper of the flame of the
Illinois History and Lincoln Collections
at the University of Illinois Library

CONTENTS

Foreword   ix
Guy C. Fraker

Preface   xi

Introduction: Did Abraham Lincoln Meet Joseph Smith?   1

FOREWORD

Here I have lived a quarter of a century and have passed from a young to an old man.

—Abraham Lincoln, February 11, 1861

FEW AMERICANS HAVE DEMONSTRATED THE COMBINATION OF ambition and selflessness, integrity and pragmatism, confidence and humility, and persistent pursuit of that which is right as did Abraham Lincoln. It is one of those incredibly fortunate instances in our history where the right man was there at the right time. Lincoln understood, as perhaps no one else, the stakes in the Civil War. It was not merely the Union at stake; it was also the very institution of democracy. Where did he get the qualities and skills it took to steer the nation and democracy through this crisis?

The major portion of his training for this task was in central Illinois. Little has been written about his life and development from when he arrived in the year of his 21st birthday until his departure for the White House 31 years later. The frontier of central Illinois was the perfect place for this rawboned farmhand to hone his natural talent and intellectual skills to meet the challenges that the nation would face.

Lincoln and the region evolved on parallel courses, maturing together. The coming of the railroads some 20 years after his arrival totally changed the region. He learned to deal with change and the revolutionary transformation of society that took place there in the 1850s. He traveled extensively across the region, first by horse and then by train, practicing law and pursuing politics. There are numerous sites, buildings, homes, streetscapes, and landscapes in the towns that he visited and the prairies that he crossed. This region felt the presence and influence of Lincoln. It, in turn, influenced and molded him.

An in-depth understanding of this enigmatic, iconic figure cannot be reached without becoming acquainted with the region and Lincoln's role in it. The political and social forces of the era made Illinois a key state in the 1850s. At that time, central Illinois was the state's most vital area. Lincoln gained the Republican nomination for president because he built the network to do so while traveling central Illinois.

The Abraham Lincoln National Heritage Area was created by Congress in 2008 and is affiliated with the National Park Service. The Area preserves the life and times of Abraham Lincoln in central Illinois. This 42-county area is a nationally significant landscape and network of sites associated with the social, cultural, economic, and political complexities of the antebellum period of our nation's history. The Looking for Lincoln Heritage Coalition coordinates projects, programs, and events that focus on telling the unique stories of the Area, enhancing and promoting Lincoln scholarship, heritage tourism, and stimulating economic development within the region.

This effort includes the publication of a shelf of books examining Lincoln's development and rise during his time in central Illinois. It is our intent that these publications will enhance the Looking for Lincoln Heritage Coalition's efforts to

- create engaging experiences that connect places and stories throughout the heritage area and promote public awareness of the region's history, culture, and significance;
- promote heritage, cultural, and recreational tourism and related heritage development that support increased economic activity and investment in heritage resources; and
- raise public consciousness about the needs and benefits of preserving the historic and cultural legacies of central Illinois.

It is my hope that you are inspired to learn more about the life, times, and legacy of Abraham Lincoln in central Illinois and the people, places, and forces in the region that shaped and elevated him to the White House.

Guy C. Fraker
Chairman of the Looking for Lincoln Heritage Coalition

PREFACE

ABRAHAM LINCOLN'S MID-19TH-CENTURY WORLD WAS ALSO

the world of Joseph Smith, Brigham Young, and the "pioneer generation" of Latter-day Saints (commonly known as Mormons). Even though Lincoln and the Mormons inhabited different political, social, and cultural circles, their stories intersected in many surprising ways. People who played important roles in Lincoln's rise to political prominence in the 1850s earlier played significant roles in the Illinois Mormon story of the 1840s. Later, the mutual awareness of Lincoln and the Latter-day Saints reached new heights as Lincoln and Brigham Young navigated the treacherous political shoals of the American Civil War.

From 1839 to 1846 the Mississippi River town of Nauvoo in Hancock County, Illinois, was the main gathering place for Latter-day Saints. But Mormons were also found farther afield. Indeed, Lincoln-history and Mormon-history storylines crossed and crisscrossed in the lives of numerous individuals and at various locations across Illinois' historical landscape. Helping people discover and explore these interconnections became an early goal of the Looking for Lincoln Heritage Coalition.

Following the initial success of the Coalition's wayside storyboard exhibit program in downtown Springfield, Illinois, I prepared similar storyboards for the western region of the Abraham Lincoln National Heritage Area that would provide a story trail for visitors traveling between historic Mormon Nauvoo and the major Lincoln historic sites in Springfield. Each storyboard included both a Lincoln story and a Mormon story that were connected in some way through historical characters and location. Funding challenges ultimately curtailed the program. Most of the storyboards were never made. Those communities that did produce storyboards focused almost exclusively on Lincoln stories. Only a handful included Mormon story connections.

This book reproduces the interconnected storylines as originally written. At many locations visitors will not find storyboards. But using the maps and stories in this book, they can imagine the Illinois landscape as it appeared to Abraham Lincoln and the early Mormons who lived and traveled across what is today the Abraham Lincoln National Heritage Area. For "armchair travelers" reading at home, the stories need not be read in any particular order, nor in extended sittings. Rather, they can be sampled and enjoyed as time permits.

I acknowledge my former colleagues at the Abraham Lincoln Presidential Library and old friends in the Looking for Lincoln Heritage Coalition who helped to make this book possible. All proceeds from this book go to the Coalition for use in the Abraham Lincoln National Heritage Area.

Bryon C. Andreasen

LOOKING FOR LINCOLN IN ILLINOIS

INTRODUCTION: DID ABRAHAM LINCOLN MEET JOSEPH SMITH?

To commemorate the 2005 bicentennial of Joseph Smith's birth, I was invited to speak in the Hall of the Representatives at the Old State Capitol in downtown Springfield, Illinois. My topic was Mormon connections to Lincoln-era Springfield. Beyond marking the bicentennial, my purpose was to raise awareness among local Latter-day Saints and members of the general public about the richness of Springfield's Mormon history. During the decade since, I have received numerous requests for copies of the address. It was intended for a general audience and serves as an introduction to provide historical context for the stories that follow. I have slightly revised and updated it for publication here.

"Land of Lincoln" is the inscription on the Illinois quarter minted in 2003 as part of the commemorative U.S. statehood quarter series. The focal image in the coin's

Abraham Lincoln (1809–65), sixteenth president of the United States.

Joseph Smith Jr. (1805–44), founding prophet of the Latter-day Saints.
Courtesy Community of Christ.

Illinois' commemorative design for the U.S. Mint's 50 State Quarters Program.

artistic design is the iconic physique of Abraham Lincoln. It is based on a famous sculpture that sits atop a granite base outside the visitors' center at Lincoln's New Salem State Historic Site, near Petersburg, Illinois. The sculpture depicts Lincoln in the vigor of early manhood—in transition from son of the wilderness, with ax in one hand, to aspiring lawyer and leader, with a voluminous book in the other. An inscription on the granite base acknowledges that the Sons of the Utah Pioneers (predominantly members of the Church of Jesus Christ of Latter-day Saints) commissioned and paid for the New Salem sculpture. The distinguished sculptor who created the work, Avard T. Fairbanks, was a Church member. Bryant Hinckley, the father of former Church president Gordon B. Hinckley, dedicated the statue at New Salem in June 1953.[1]

The New Salem image of Lincoln has become a symbol of the state of Illinois. But it also fittingly symbolizes the often unknown or forgotten connections between the Mormon people and the Springfield area during the Lincoln era. Usually when people think of the Mormons and Illinois, they think of Nauvoo. But the story is much larger. It extends far beyond Nauvoo and Hancock County—all the way to Illinois' capital city, the hometown of Abraham Lincoln.

Gordon B. Hinckley (1910–2008) himself provided a link back to Lincoln-era Springfield. His grandfather, Ira Nathaniel Hinckley, was in his teens and living in Springfield around the time Lincoln was courting Mary Todd in the early 1840s.[2] Like Lincoln, young Ira Hinckley apparently had a natural bent for mechanical things and hands-on work, especially blacksmithing. He eventually joined the Latter-day Saints and found himself in Nauvoo. But not before he may have witnessed some interesting events regarding the Latter-day Saints in the Springfield area.[3]

EARLY CROSSINGS

In the autumn of 1830—only a few months after 24-year-old Joseph Smith Jr. published the *Book of Mormon* and organized the Church of Christ (as it was originally named) in upstate New York, and at the same time that 21-year-old Abraham Lincoln was ferrying across the Wabash River with his father's family on their move from Indiana to Illinois—Mormon missionaries were traveling through the southern counties of Illinois preaching the restored gospel on their way to the Indian territories on Missouri's western border. In the summer of 1831, while Lincoln was floating down the Mississippi River on Denton Offutt's flatboat and later establishing himself as a resident of New Salem, the Pratt brothers—Parley and Orson—and other Mormon missionaries were preaching and baptizing in counties surrounding Springfield as they passed to and from the newly revealed land of Zion in Missouri.[4]

ZION'S CAMP

In the spring of 1834, Joseph Smith started out from the Mormon community of Kirtland, Ohio, leading a relief expedition to the Missouri Saints who had been driven from their homes. The company —known as Zion's Camp—consisted of around 200 armed men traveling by foot and horseback. It took the main company four weeks to reach a spot just west of Decatur, Illinois. There they tarried long enough to hold a mock battle. Then on Friday, May 30, Zion's Camp approached Springfield. Joseph Smith was apprehensive about how the Mormons might be treated by the people in Springfield, so he sent his counselor Frederick G. Williams ahead into town to see if it would be safe to pass through and purchase supplies.[5]

Avard Fairbank's heroic statue of Lincoln, at New Salem State Historic Site near Petersburg, was commissioned by the Sons of the Utah Pioneers as a gift to the state of Illinois.

The Springfield newspaper at the time, the *Sangamo Journal*, made note of Zion's Camp shortly after it passed through. The paper reported that the company was composed of able-bodied men who were generally armed. One of the group *"who appeared to be a leader"* said that *"he had himself performed more miracles than were recorded in the Old and New Testaments."*[6] Joseph Smith's history merely records that *"the people were somewhat excited, more from a curiosity to know where we were going than from a desire to hinder us."*[7] This appears to be the first time the Mormon prophet was in the Springfield vicinity.

Springfield was not the state capital at the time, however. There was no majestic capitol building standing in the middle of town. And Abraham Lincoln still lived in New Salem. No surviving records suggest that Lincoln was in Springfield on May 30, 1834. Instead, he almost certainly was in New Salem, some 27 miles northwest of Springfield.[8] It is highly unlikely that he would have had an opportunity to meet Joseph Smith as Zion's Camp passed through the area.

Three years later, Lincoln moved to Springfield, which the state legislature had recently designated as Illinois' new capital city. Construction began on a new capitol building. By the next time Mormons came to the area in large numbers, Springfield was a bigger, busier place—and Lincoln was a resident.

KIRTLAND CAMP

That next time was in September 1838, when a company of several hundred Latter-day Saints known as Kirtland Camp passed through on their way to the new Mormon headquarters at Far West, Missouri. A fair number of this group, including the future Springfield stake president, Edwin P. Merriam, remained behind in the Springfield area, temporarily too sick or exhausted to go on.[9] One member of the group wrote, shortly after passing through Springfield,

> *We could not procure anything for our teams to eat and were obliged to fasten them to our wagons and give them a little corn or turn them onto dry prairie almost destitute of vegetation. Springfield is destined to be the seat of government of Illinois and the state house is now in course of building. It is situated on a beautiful prairie and looks like a flourishing place though it is yet in its infancy.*[10]

That winter, when the main body of Mormons was driven out of Missouri and fled to Illinois for safety, there was already a good number of Mormons living in Sangamon County as a result of Kirtland Camp having come through the previous autumn.[11]

PASSING APOSTLES

Church apostle (and future Church president) Wilford Woodruff stayed the winter of 1838–39 with his family just north of Rochester, a village east of Springfield (only a few miles from the current Springfield, Illinois, LDS Church Stake Center). He presided at a conference of Springfield area church members in March 1839, before moving his family to join the bulk of the Mormon refugees from Missouri who were congregating in and around the Mississippi River town of Quincy, Illinois.[12]

In October 1839, apostles Brigham Young and Heber C. Kimball stayed in Springfield on their journey to England to preside over missionary work there. They were ill when they left their families behind at Nauvoo.[13] They were fortunate to find rooms in Springfield with church members because the city's hotels and inns were filled to bursting with politicians from all over Illinois. The Whig political party was having its first ever statewide convention. While Brigham Young and Heber Kimball languished in their sickbeds trying to recuperate to go on to England, the rising Whig politician Abraham Lincoln was a few blocks away busily politicking on behalf of future presidential candidate William Henry Harrison.[14] Convention delegates chose Lincoln to be one of the Whig presidential electors. Ironically, the next year the Mormon vote in Nauvoo would go overwhelmingly for Harrison, but elector Lincoln would have his name scratched from the ballot by 200 Mormon voters in Nauvoo who replaced it with that of Judge James H. Ralston, a Democrat from Quincy, Illinois.[15]

JOSEPH SMITH PASSES THROUGH

That same autumn of 1839, a month after Brigham Young and Heber C. Kimball spent their week in Springfield, Joseph Smith passed through the area for the second time, this time on his way to Washington, D.C., to seek relief from Congress and President Martin Van Buren for Mormon property losses in Missouri. The Prophet stopped in Springfield to greet church members and to consult with politicians on ways to appeal to the president and Congress. He stayed at Brother John Snider's home for four days. *"I preached several times while here,"* Joseph Smith later related. *"General James Adams, judge of probate, heard of me, sought me out, and took me home with him, and treated me like a father."*[16] James Adams—one of Springfield's earliest settlers, a prominent Democrat, and a political champion of the young, up-and-coming politician Stephen A. Douglas—lived at the southwest corner of Fourth Street and Jefferson (part of the Amtrak railway depot parking lot today).[17] General Adams's involvement with the Mormons would grow.

DID LINCOLN MEET THE PROPHET IN 1839?

Did Abraham Lincoln meet Joseph Smith sometime during the four days that the Prophet was in Springfield from November 4 to 8, 1839? Legal records show that Lincoln was in Springfield during those days working away in his law office, which at that time was on the second floor of a building that was part of Hoffman's Row on Fifth Street, just northwest of the public square where the state capitol building was being erected.[18] Lincoln's law partner, John Todd Stuart, was the U.S. congressman from the region. Stuart had left for Washington just two days before Joseph Smith arrived in town; otherwise they might have traveled to Washington together (an intriguing circumstance that sets the historical imagination to wondering how things might have been had events unfolded that way). As it is, Lincoln wrote Stuart three months later, remarking, *"Joshua Speed says he wrote you what Jo Smith said about you as he passed here. We will procure the names of some of his people here and send them to you before long."*[19]

What does this mean? Illinois Whigs were busy courting the favor of the Mormons, and Lincoln was trying to help Stuart solidify support from local voters. Unfortunately, it does not appear that either Joshua Speed's letter or the follow-up letter to Stuart have survived. Joshua Speed was Lincoln's closest friend in Springfield. They roomed together in the top of Speed's store. If Joshua Speed talked to Joseph Smith, it is highly likely that Abraham Lincoln did as well—though there is nothing definitive to prove it.

PASSAGE OF THE NAUVOO CHARTER

A year later in Springfield (June 1840), the notorious militia general and political gadfly John C. Bennett first connected to the Mormons. *"I attended the meeting of your people opposite Mr. Lowery's hotel, but did not make myself known, as I had no personal acquaintance in the congregation,"* he wrote Joseph Smith in Nauvoo.[20] The controversial Bennett earned great favor among the Mormons by shepherding the Nauvoo charter through the state legislature in Springfield the following December.

The capitol building was in the final stages of completion in December 1840. The Illinois Senate was meeting in its new chambers on the second floor of the new building, but the Illinois House of Representatives had not yet moved into its new spacious hall opposite the Senate chamber. The House was still convening in the wood-frame Methodist Church on the corner of Fifth and Monroe Streets (where the Edwards Building stands today). It was from the window of the Methodist Church that state representative Abraham Lincoln made an inglorious leap out the window (to prevent a legislative quorum) for which he received much ridicule.[21] That was on Saturday, December 5. The next Monday, December 7, the House met in their new capitol quarters for the first time.[22] It was there, on Thursday, December 10, that the Senate bill granting Nauvoo a city charter was first introduced in the House. Two days later, on Saturday, December 12, 1840, the Illinois House of Representatives passed the Nauvoo charter by voice vote with only a very few nay votes sounded.[23]

One of the yes votes was voiced by Abraham Lincoln. Writing to Joseph Smith on December 16, 1840—the day Governor Thomas Carlin signed the charter bill—John C. Bennett mentioned in the course of his report this interesting point: *"Here I should not forget to mention, that Lincoln whose name we erased from the electoral ticket in November had the magnanimity to vote for our act, and came forward, after the final vote to the bar of the house, and cordially congratulated me on its passage."*[24] Bennett named other prominent legislators of both parties who supported the charter. Several years later, when the Mormon cause became extremely unpopular, especially among members of Lincoln's Whig party, these votes became an embarrassment.

For those steeped in Lincoln lore, it is interesting to note that the Nauvoo charter vote came during a personally troubling time for Lincoln—just a few days after his infamous "leaping" episode in the House of Representatives and just a few days before Lincoln allegedly broke a marriage engagement to Mary Todd.[25]

A STAKE FOR SPRINGFIELD

Though late 1840 may have been a tough time for Abraham Lincoln, it was an exciting time for local Latter-day Saints. A month before the legislature passed the Nauvoo charter, Church leaders from Nauvoo led by the Prophet's brother, Hyrum Smith, came to town and organized the members of the vicinity into a stake.[26] Their visit was part of a larger effort to organize stakes throughout west central Illinois. Hyrum Smith organized the first Springfield stake of the Church of Jesus Christ of Latter-day Saints on Thursday, November 5, 1840—just two days before the presidential election. Edwin P. Merriam was called to serve as the president of the stake, with Isaac H. Bishop and Arnold Stephens as counselors. Also organized was a local Bishop's Court, with Abraham Palmer, Henry Stephens, and Jonathan Palmer called as members.[27]

SPRINGFIELD'S JAMES ADAMS

Church membership continued to grow in the Springfield area. The *Sangamo Journal* on May 14, 1841, reported, *"The Church of the Latter Day Saints will hold Divine Worship to day, at their usual place of meeting, in the west part of the city."*[28]

One of the more important Springfield converts was the local probate judge James Adams. Students of Abraham Lincoln will recognize Adams as the target of Lincoln's scathing personal attacks in what are known as the "Sampson's Ghost Letters."[29] In 1837 Adams had run as the Democratic candidate for county probate judge against Lincoln's good friend the Whig candidate Dr. Anson G. Henry. It was a rough campaign. During the summer run-up to the August election, Lincoln made newspaper allegations that Adams had cheated a widow out of her property[30] and later declared that Adams previously fled New York on account of a forgery charge. At the time Adams was an officer in the First Christian Church of Springfield, and an anonymous letter to the newspaper derided Adams's religiosity, stating that Adams's alleged bad deeds could not be *"covered over by the mantle of religion."*[31] Adams hotly denied all charges and deeply resented his attacker hiding behind a pseudonym. All this played out in the pages of the local newspaper. Adams won the election by a large majority, and a somewhat chastened Lincoln learned that at least in this instance, negative political attacks did not pay off. Lincoln would be more circumspect in the future.[32]

As previously noted, Adams had met Joseph Smith in Springfield in November 1839. At least partly because Adams was about the age of Joseph Smith's father, Joseph seemed to relate to Adams as a kind of surrogate father after his own father died at Nauvoo on September 14, 1840. Adams was among those who were present as the Prophet revealed elements of the endowment ceremony that would later be practiced in Latter-day Saint temples. His visits to Nauvoo increased in frequency and duration over time.[33]

FROM A STAKE TO A BRANCH

At the end of May 1841, Joseph Smith dissolved all outlying stakes and requested church members to relocate to Hancock County.[34] This ended the short existence of the original Springfield Illinois Stake. Over the next year, many of the local church members packed up and moved. Stake President Edwin Merriam, for example, relocated to Nauvoo. Not all church members moved, however. A church presence in the capital city was still deemed important. So, on January 25, 1842, the defunct Springfield stake was reorganized into a branch (the smallest ecclesiastical administrative unit in the Church), and James Adams became the branch president.

NEGATIVE PRESS

In the summer of 1842, John C. Bennett turned against the Church and published a series of explosive exposés in Springfield's Whig newspaper, the *Sangamo Journal*. He charged Mormon leaders with political and economic tyranny, and with instituting a secret system of "spiritual wifery"—describing with lurid exaggeration the practice of plural marriage that had been privately introduced as a sacred religious principle to some Latter-day Saints by Joseph Smith.[35]

In this same summer of 1842, Abraham Lincoln was secretly courting Mary Todd in the parlor of the very home of the Whig newspaper editor who was publishing all the Bennett attacks.[36] What did Abraham Lincoln think about the negative turn Whig newspapers were taking against the Mormons? The only evidence that has ever come to light is a sentence in a letter Lincoln wrote to an attorney in Shawneetown in southern Illinois in July 1842. He wrote, *"There is nothing new here. Bennett's Mormon disclosures are making some little stir here, but not very great."*[37] Knowing Lincoln's often ribald sense of humor, it is probable that Joseph Smith and the Mormons may have been the butt of some risqué jokes. But because he knew full well by personal experience that reports published in the politically partisan newspapers of the day were often exaggerated accounts designed to discredit opponents, he probably did not take Bennett's reports too seriously. If so, he underestimated the long-term impact of Bennett's slanders, for Illinois Whig politicians would put to good use Bennett's attacks in the months ahead.[38]

In Springfield, James Adams was instrumental in countering damage to the Latter-day Saints in Democratic circles. He remained steadfastly loyal to Joseph Smith. But soon warrants were issued for the arrest of the Mormon prophet, and church members in Springfield became vital to keeping leaders in Nauvoo apprised of what was going on.[39]

ATTEMPTS AT EXTRADITION

On May 6, 1842, someone tried to assassinate former Missouri governor Lilburn Boggs (signer of the infamous "extermination order" precipitating the expulsion of the Mormons from Missouri in the winter of 1839). Missourians captured the Mormon frontiersman Orrin Porter Rockwell and charged him with attempted murder. A Missouri grand jury also indicted Joseph Smith as an accomplice to attempted murder. Missouri's governor formally requested Illinois governor Thomas Carlin to arrest Joseph Smith and extradite him to Missouri for trial.

The Mormon prophet, having already been incarcerated in a Missouri jail for one long, cold winter, was convinced he could receive no justice in a Missouri courtroom and went into hiding. Leading Illinois lawyers and politicians discussed the case in Springfield and came to the conclusion that grounds for extradition were exceedingly weak—that Joseph Smith had not been present in the state of Missouri at the time of the attempted murder, and that Missouri was incapable of assuring proper legal process in the case.[40]

PRELIMINARY MEETINGS

On December 13, 1842, Hyrum Smith and Apostle Willard Richards (one of two men who would survive the murderous assault on Joseph and Hyrum Smith in the Carthage jail two years later) arrived in Springfield in company with seven others. Their mission was to explore the topic of Missouri's extradition request and to seek debt relief from the federal court. Richards recorded that he put up in the Globe Tavern.[41] This is the same Globe Tavern where Abraham Lincoln and Mary Todd Lincoln had spent their wedding night a month earlier, and where they were still residing when Elder Richards stayed there. Did some of the Mormon visitors and the Lincolns eat at the same boarding table together? It is possible, but unknown for certain.

At the time, William Smith—Joseph's younger brother—was serving in the Illinois House of Representatives as a legislator from Hancock County. Willard Richards met with William Smith and James Adams and other Mormons, but more important, he also conferred with the new governor, Thomas Ford, Illinois supreme court justice Stephen A. Douglas, and Illinois secretary of state Lyman Trumbull (the same Lyman Trumbull who would defeat Lincoln for a seat in the U.S. Senate a decade later). Willard Richards visited the capitol building, where he observed proceedings in both the House and Senate chambers, and where he met with state senator James H. Ralston from Quincy, Illinois, and judge Stephen A. Douglas,

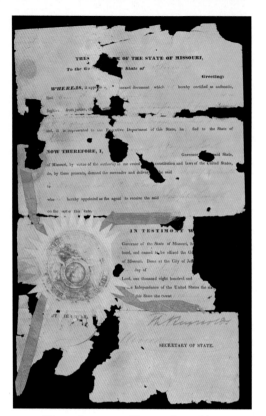

who was hearing cases in the capitol's Supreme Court chamber. He also visited the U.S. district attorney for Illinois, Justin Butterfield (who a few years later would win out over Abraham Lincoln in a patronage fight for an appointment from President Zachary Taylor as commissioner of the General Land Office in Washington, D.C.). The result of all these discussions was a consensus among the judges, lawyers, and politicians that Missouri's extradition writ against Joseph Smith was deficient; that he ought to voluntarily surrender to arrest and come to Springfield for a habeas corpus hearing during which he would almost certainly succeed in quashing the writ.

Missouri governor Thomas Reynolds, a former Illinois supreme court judge, issued this writ of extradition requesting that Joseph Smith be arrested and returned to Missouri for trial.

THE PROPHET RETURNS TO SPRINGFIELD

So, on Friday, December 30, 1842, Joseph Smith entered Springfield for the last time. He arrived with an entourage of Mormon leaders after a four-day winter journey from Nauvoo.[42] He stayed with James Adams, reporting that he slept on Adams's couch.[43] The next morning, New Year's Eve, Joseph Smith permitted himself to be arrested and then petitioned for a writ of habeas corpus before the U.S. district court judge Nathaniel Pope in the federal courtroom on the second floor of the Tinsley Building—which today is the location of the Lincoln-Herndon Law Office State Historic Site. In December 1842, however, Lincoln's law office was not in the Tinsley Building; he did not move there until a few months later, in the summer of 1843.[44]

Representing Joseph were U.S. district attorney Justin Butterfield and his new law partner, Benjamin Edwards. Edwards was the youngest son in the politically prominent, Springfield-based Edwards family (and brother-in-law to Mary Lincoln's sister, Elizabeth Edwards). Opposing them was Illinois attorney general Josiah Lamborn (who three years later would unsuccessfully prosecute the accused assassins of Joseph Smith).

After the Prophet's lawyers presented his habeas corpus petition before the court, Judge Pope scheduled Joseph Smith's case for opening motions on Monday morning January 2, 1843. Then, as Joseph Smith was going down the hall stairway to leave the building, several rowdies in the street started to swear and shout insults. Some pushing and shoving ensued between members of the crowd and Mormon officials Hyrum Smith and Wilson Law at the foot of the stairs as they tried to enter onto the street. The federal marshal had to quickly intervene to prevent a mob scene.[45]

The Prophet made his way across the street to pay his respects to Governor Thomas Ford, who was ill and quartered in the American House, the nicest hotel in the city (which was directly across the street from the Tinsley Building). Joseph then had lunch with his attorney Justin Butterfield in the American House. By 2 p.m. he was back safely at Judge Adams's house.[46] His journal records that later that afternoon a team of horses *ran away, and went past the state house, when the hue-and-cry was raised, 'Joe Smith is running away!,' which produced great excitement and a sudden adjournment of the House of Representatives.*[47]

SENATOR BREESE'S NEW YEAR'S EVE
GALA AT THE AMERICAN HOUSE

That night the newly elected U.S. senator Sidney Breese held a huge celebration party at the American House (he had just defeated fellow Democrat Stephen A. Douglas in the senatorial election held in the Illinois General Assembly). According to Lincoln historian Harry Pratt, Joseph Smith attended the party that New Year's Eve at the American House, but Pratt's evidence is unclear.[48] The party is described in a newspaper report, but there is no mention of Joseph Smith being there.[49] Neither is it mentioned in any Mormon sources.

This did not stop the novelist Irving Stone from imaging a remarkable scene in his historical romance *Love Is Eternal*, about the courtship and marriage of Abraham and Mary Lincoln. He places the Lincolns at the New Year's Eve party at the American House. In the scene as depicted in the novel, Joseph Smith enters the room and creates an immediate sensation. Mary makes her way over to him and is introduced. Then,

Mary found herself gazing into a pair of the most magnetic blue eyes she had ever encountered. . . . "May I bid you welcome to Springfield, Mr. Smith?" she said, "Most of us feel you are being persecuted." "Thank you, Mrs. Lincoln," the Prophet replied. His voice a powerful throbbing organ. . . . [He] flashed her a taunting smile. "Mrs. Lincoln, if ever you become disillusioned with your chosen church . . . come to Nauvoo and let me reveal the true religion to you." "Thank you," she replied with a full curtsy, "it's always gratifying to be wanted."[50]

Did the Lincolns really meet Joseph Smith at the Sidney Breese levy at the American House on New Year's Eve 1842? There appears to be no evidence to substantiate a meeting, but no one knows for sure.

MORMON SERMONS IN THE OLD STATE CAPITOL

On Sunday morning, New Year's Day, Samuel Hackleton, Speaker of the Illinois House of Representatives, arrived at the James Adams residence to invite Joseph Smith to preach in the Hall of the Representatives.[51] A huge crowd descended on the state capitol building in hopes of hearing the Mormon prophet preach a sermon. Instead, Joseph asked one of the church's apostles, Orson Hyde (recently returned from a trip to Europe and the Holy Land) to speak. Later that afternoon, Apostle John Taylor—who would become the third president of the Church, following Brigham Young—preached in the same spacious hall, with Joseph in the audience.[52] People were disappointed that the Prophet did not speak, but his mere presence seemed to cause excitement enough. A correspondent for a Quincy, Illinois, newspaper wrote, *"I have been to preaching in the Representative Chamber, and have heard an ingenious and eloquent discourse from the Mormon Elder Hyde. The hall was crowded, Joseph Smith being the great lion of the day."*[53]

THE PROPHET'S SPRINGFIELD HABEAS CORPUS HEARING

On Monday morning, January 2, 1843, the courtroom was packed with spectators. Attorney General Lamborn requested a postponement until Wednesday morning (in part to accommodate his assignment to oppose attorney Abraham Lincoln in a legislative proceeding at the statehouse). Attorney Butterfield filed some affidavits on behalf of Joseph Smith. Judge Pope then rescheduled the hearing for the morning of Wednesday, January 4, and adjourned the proceeding; the disappointed spectators disbursed.

Joseph Smith's habeas corpus proceedings ended up taking portions of three days—Monday, Wednesday, and Thursday (January 2, 4, and 5). The result was a decision by Judge Pope to quash the writ of extradition and to set Joseph Smith free. No one was surprised.[54]

Unusual throughout the entire proceedings was the presence of so many women in the courtroom. The attending U.S. marshal, William Prentiss, told the visiting Mormons that it was the first time since he had become marshal that ladies attended court proceedings.[55] It seems that anyone who was anyone in Springfield society attended the trial at one time or another, including Judge Pope's daughter,[56] a daughter of Joseph's lawyer Justin Butterfield, and Mary Lincoln. At the time Mary was a young bride of two months, and two months pregnant. But her delicate condition apparently did not keep her away from the proceedings. Indeed, the Joseph Smith hearing was as much a Springfield social event as it was a legal and political event.[57]

The historical source placing Mary Lincoln in attendance at the trial is a speech given by a former Illinois congressman and political associate of Abraham Lincoln's, Isaac N. Arnold. In remarks delivered before the Bar Association of the State of Illinois in January 1881 at Springfield, Arnold reminisced at length about the celebrated Joseph Smith hearing:

> *The Court-Room was thronged with prominent members of the bar, and public men. Judge Pope was a gallant gentleman of the old school, and loved nothing better than to be in the midst of youth and beauty. Seats were crowded on the Judge's platform, on both sides, and behind the Judge, and an array of brilliant and beautiful ladies almost encircled the Court. Mr. Butterfield, dressed á la Webster, in blue dress-coat and metal buttons, with buff vest, rose with dignity, and amidst the most profound silence. Pausing and running his eyes admiringly from the central figure of Judge Pope, along the rows of lovely women on each side of him, he said:*
>
> > *"May it please the Court, I appear before you to-day under circumstances most novel and peculiar. I am to address the 'Pope' (bowing to the Judge) surrounded by angels (bowing still lower to the ladies), in the presence of the holy Apostles, in behalf of the Prophet of the Lord."*[58]

During the hearing, amateur artist Benjamin West did a pencil sketch from life of Joseph Smith. The original sketch is in the possession of the Abraham Lincoln Presidential Library and is occasionally displayed on rotation in the gallery in the "Ghosts of the Library" waiting area at the Abraham Lincoln Presidential Museum.

Arnold specifically names *"Mrs. Lincoln"* as being *"[a]mong the most lovely and attractive"* of the *"angels"* in attendance. But did her husband, Abraham Lincoln, also attend the proceedings? Arnold may be interpreted to suggest that he did. After listing some of the women (including Mary Lincoln) who attended, he concluded his remarks about the Joseph Smith hearing with the observation that *"the chief actors in that drama"* had by 1881 *"nearly all passed away."* He continued:

The genial and learned Judge, the prisoner, and his able counselor, so full of wit and humor, the eloquent Attorney-General, the Governors of both States, the Marshal and Clerk, and nearly all of the distinguished lawyers and public men, Lincoln, Logan, Judge Breese, Baker, *and others, who laughed and joked so merrily over the happy allusions of Mr. Butterfield, have passed away.* (emphasis added)[59]

Arnold is not specific about which session of the multiday hearing proceedings the *"distinguished lawyers and public men"* (including Lincoln) may have attended. Records indicate that for much of the week Lincoln was involved at the statehouse serving as defense attorney for Illinois supreme court justice Thomas C. Browne, who was being investigated for removal. A comparison of Lincoln's removal hearing schedule and Joseph Smith's habeas corpus hearing schedule reveals that it may have been possible for Lincoln to have been present on Wednesday morning, January 4 (when Lamborn and Butterfield presented their main arguments), and Thursday morning, January 5, when Judge Pope delivered his opinion and final decision. But historians may never know for sure whether Lincoln was actually present during any of the court proceedings.[60]

OTHER SOCIAL GATHERINGS

The *History of the Church* has Joseph relating, *"I received many invitations to visit distinguished gentlemen in Springfield, which time would not permit me to comply with."*[61] Was Lincoln among those whose invitations could not be accepted? Alternatively, could Lincoln have been among those unnamed individuals who met Joseph Smith outside the court hearing? The names of three dozen individuals (not counting Church members) are recorded in Joseph's journal as having met the Prophet over the course of the week. Lincoln's name is not among them.

Joseph Smith's journal records two instances where several unnamed individuals visited the Prophet. One was late in the afternoon on Monday, January 2, when Josiah Lamborn, William Prentiss, and *"some ½ dozen others"* called on Joseph at the home of James Adams. The other was a dinner party hosted by U.S. marshal William Prentiss at his home on the evening of January 4. Besides the Prentiss family, Joseph's journal lists Stephen A. Douglas, Justin Butterfield, Benjamin Edwards, William Pope (Judge Nathaniel Pope's oldest son), Josiah Lamborn, and *"many others"* as attendees. Again, it is not possible at this late date to determine if Lincoln was in attendance on either occasion. Of the two, it seems less likely that he would have visited the Adams home on January 2, given Lincoln's involvement in the defense of supreme court justice Browne to be presented the next day, and the possible lingering animosity between Lincoln and Adams over the unpleasant words they exchanged during the county probate election several years earlier.

On the day before he left Springfield to return to Nauvoo, Joseph Smith met a last time with Judge Pope and other dignitaries in the Tinsley Building. It is not known if Lincoln was there, but Judge Pope's son, William Pope, was. Joseph Smith reported, *"[Judge Pope's] son wished me well, and hoped I should not be [persecuted] . . . any more. [I] blessed him."*[62]

So, did Abraham Lincoln meet and talk with Joseph Smith during that long first week in January 1843? While there are several instances where their meeting may have been plausible, it is simply not known for certain if they ever did.[63]

SEPARATE DESTINIES

On Saturday morning, January 7, 1843, Joseph Smith took his last leave of Illinois' capital city, never to return. Lincoln probably never had another opportunity to see Joseph Smith. There is no evidence that he ever visited Nauvoo. When the Prophet and his brother Hyrum were murdered in the Carthage jail, Lincoln was in Springfield deeply engaged in the presidential contest between his hero Henry Clay and dark-horse Democratic candidate James K. Polk, whose surprise nomination was what filled most of the newspaper columns at the time.[64]

In the 1850s Lincoln would point to the Mormons when goading Stephen A. Douglas on the issue of "popular sovereignty," saying that if people could vote their moral conscience to allow slavery in the territories, why shouldn't the Mormons be allowed to vote their moral conscience to have polygamy in Utah?[65] His presidential relations with the Mormons are best remembered by his story about treating Brigham Young like a tree stump in the middle of a field—it is best to just plow around it and leave it alone.[66] But in general, there is little about the Mormons in any of Lincoln's surviving papers.

Of the many Springfield residents who met the Mormon Prophet during one or more of his visits to town, most probably agreed with Governor Thomas Ford, who considered Joseph Smith to be an imposter, too corrupt to establish a religious system that could have permanent success.[67] Is that what Lincoln thought? It is impossible to know.[68] It is almost certain, however, that neither he nor any of his neighbors ever guessed that by the bicentennial of the Prophet's birth in 2005 the Church that Joseph Smith founded would have over 12 million members, the majority of whom would be living outside North America, and that the *Book of Mormon* would be published in tens of millions of copies in over 120 different languages.

With the perspective of 200 years, the prominent scholar of Jacksonian America Robert Remini (no Mormon himself) proclaimed that Joseph Smith was *"an organizing genius"* and *"a man of little formal education but of striking intellectual power . . . whose religious writings have influenced millions of people around the world."*[69]

The celebrated Jewish scholar of American culture Harold Bloom has declared that *"Smith's genius for restoration exceeded that of even Muhammad"* and that *"as an authentic religious genius . . . [he] surpassed all Americans before or since."*[70]

Joseph Smith himself recorded that the angel Moroni had told him that his *"name should be had for good and evil among all nations, kindreds, and tongues, or that it should be both good and evil spoken of among all people."*[71] After more than 200 years since his birth, that seems to be at least one prophecy with which no one can quibble.

NOTES

1. Eugene F. Fairbanks, "Sculptural Commemorations of Abraham Lincoln by Avard T. Fairbanks," *Journal of the Abraham Lincoln Association* 26, no. 2 (Summer 2005): 49–74, at 52–55. See also Eugene F. Fairbanks, *Abraham Lincoln Sculpture Created by Avard T. Fairbanks* (Bellingham, Wash.: Fairbanks Arts and Books, 2002), 40–50, 52.

2. For many years, a standard account of the Lincoln-Todd courtship has been chapters 3–6 in Ruth Painter Randall, *Mary Lincoln: Biography of a Marriage* (Boston: Little, Brown, 1953). But see also the accounts in Douglas L. Wilson, *Honor's Voice: The Transformation of Abraham Lincoln* (New York: Alfred A. Knopf, 1998), and Jean H. Baker, *Mary Todd Lincoln: A Biography* (New York: W. W. Norton, 1987). A more recent telling of the courtship is in Kenneth J. Winkle, *Abraham and Mary Lincoln* (Carbondale: Southern Illinois University Press, 2011). Writer Daniel Mark Epstein covers the courtship in the first four chapters of *The Lincolns: Portrait of a Marriage* (New York: Ballantine Books, 2008). But Epstein's account is more akin to historical fiction than biography, as the author takes literary license with the story by articulating the inner thoughts of the characters involved, by placing words in their mouths, and by going beyond the evidence in ways that historians are not allowed.

3. Regarding Lincoln's consideration of blacksmithing, see Lincoln's "Autobiography Written for John L. Scripps (c. June 1860)," in Roy P. Basler, ed., *The Collected Works of Abraham Lincoln*, 8 vols. (New Brunswick, N.J.: Rutgers University Press, 1953), 4:65 (hereinafter *CW*). Regarding Ira Nathaniel Hinckley, see Arden and Lorraine Ashton, compilers, *The Life and Family of Ira Nathaniel Hinckley* (Salt Lake City, Utah: Alonzo A. Hinckley Family Organization, 2000).

4. Marlene C. Kettley, Arnold K. Garr, and Craig K. Manscill, *Mormon Thoroughfare: A History of the Church in Illinois, 1830–1839* (Provo, Utah: Religious Studies Center, Brigham Young University, 2006), 3–8, 16–25; Scot Facer Proctor and Maurine Jensen Proctor, eds., *Autobiography of Parley P. Pratt* (Salt Lake City, Utah: Deseret Book, 2000), 58, 83–84; Jan Shipps and John W. Welch, eds., *The Journal of William E. McLellin, 1831–1836* (Provo, Utah: BYU Studies; Urbana: University of Illinois Press, 1994), 38–42. See also "Travel between Ohio and Missouri, 1831–1838" and "Early Missions, 1831–1844," in Brandon S. Plewe, ed., *Mapping Mormonism: An Atlas of Latter-day Saint History* (Provo, Utah: BYU Press, 2012), 38–43. Regarding the designation of Jackson County, Missouri, as the location of *"the land of promise, and the place for the city of Zion,"* see Robin Scott Jensen, Robert J. Woodford, and Steven C. Harper, eds., *The Joseph Smith Papers: Revelations and Translations, Manuscript Revelation Books*, facsimile edition (Salt Lake City, Utah: Church Historians Press, 2009), 158–61 (*Doctrine & Covenants* section 57).

5. Frederick G. Williams, *The Life of Dr. Frederick G. Williams: Counselor to the Prophet Joseph Smith* (Provo, Utah: BYU Studies, 2012), 259–60. See also Joseph Smith, *History of the Church*, 2nd ed., 8 vols. (Salt Lake City, Utah: Deseret Book, 1976), 2:76 (hereinafter *HC*).

6. "The Company of Mormons . . . ," *Sangamo Journal*, June 7, 1834, 2:6.

7. *HC*, 2:77.

8. Historians have been able to verify Lincoln's location and activities for only two dates in May 1834—May 5 at the New Salem polling place for the election of Sangamon County sheriff, and May 6 when Lincoln carried the New Salem poll book to Springfield. Earl Schenck Miers, ed., *Lincoln Day-by-Day: A Chronology, 1809–1865* (Dayton, Ohio: Morningside Press, 1991), 38. An online version, *The Lincoln Log: A Daily Chronology of the Life of Abraham Lincoln*, is maintained by the Papers of Abraham Lincoln at www.thelincolnlog.org.

9. Kettley, *Mormon Thoroughfare*, 89. Joel H. Johnson, for example, stayed behind in Springfield over the winter of 1838–39 to preside over a detachment of sick church members. Susan Session Rugh, *Our Common Country: Family Farming, Culture, and Community in the Nineteenth-Century Midwest* (Bloomington: Indiana University Press, 2001), 34.

10. *HC*, 3:139.

11. Apparently, some in Springfield already had an unfavorable opinion of Mormons by early 1839. A reflection of this is that Springfield citizens who in 1834 had funded construction of the city's first large church building, the First Christian Church (a building shared by other Protestant denominations), quickly voted to restrict use of the building to the Christian Church (Disciples of Christ) to foreclose the possibility that Mormons might use the building. John E. Washington, *They Knew Lincoln* (New York: E. P. Dutton & Co., 1942), 199–200.

12. Thomas G. Alexander, *Things in Heaven and Earth: The Life and Times of Wilford Woodruff, a Mormon Prophet* (Salt Lake City, Utah: Signature Books, 1991), 76, 78, 81–83.

13. Elders Young and Kimball were in Springfield from Saturday, October 5, to Friday, October 11, 1839. They were still ill at the end of their weeklong stay, and had to lie on the floor of the wagon that conveyed them out of the city. *HC*, 4:11, 14–15.

14. The Whig state convention was held in Springfield on October 7–8, 1839. Miers, *Lincoln Day-by-Day*, 117–18. Regarding the Whig convention, see Richard Lawrence Miller, *Lincoln and His World: Prairie Politician, 1834–1842* (Mechanicsburg, Penn.: Stackpole Books, 2008), 328–29. Young and Kimball returned to Springfield briefly and preached in the autumn of 1842 as part of a mission assignment to counteract anti-Mormon propaganda circulating throughout Illinois. See Leonard J. Arrington, *Brigham Young: American Moses* (New York: Alfred A. Knopf, 1985), 103–4; Stanley B. Kimball, *Heber C. Kimball: Mormon Patriarch and Pioneer* (Urbana, Ill., 1981), 99, 103.

15. Dallin H. Oaks and Marvin S. Hill, *Carthage Conspiracy: The Trial of the Accused Assassins of Joseph Smith* (Urbana: University of Illinois Press, 1975), 92–93, note 12. An erroneous report in some secondary accounts suggests it was the future president's first cousin, also named Abraham Lincoln, a resident of eastern Hancock County, Illinois, who was the elector whose name Nauvoo voters scratched from their ballots in 1840. This is incorrect. Hancock County's Abraham Lincoln did not attend the state convention in Springfield that picked the 1840 Whig presidential electors, and Whig ballots distinctly list *"Abram Lincoln of Sangamon,"* not Hancock County (other electors were from Cook, Gallatin, McDonough, and White counties). See, for example, Hancock County's Whig newspaper *The Western World* (published in Warsaw), September 16, 1840. Moreover, John C. Bennett's December 16, 1840, letter to Joseph Smith confirms that it was Abraham Lincoln the

state legislator (Hancock County's Abraham Lincoln never served in the state legislature), whose name the Mormons scratched. Bennett's letter was published in *Times and Season* (Nauvoo, Illinois) vol. 2, no. 5, January 1, 1841, at pp. 266–67. See also *HC*, 4: 248–49.

16. Joseph Smith arrived in Springfield on Monday, November 4, 1839, in company with Sidney Rigdon, Elias Higbee, Orrin Porter Rockwell, and Dr. Robert D. Foster. A company led by William Law that was journeying from Canada to Nauvoo fortuitously met the Prophet's party near Springfield and stayed with them in town over the next three days. Everyone left on Friday, November 8—the Prophet's party continuing its journey east, William Law's party continuing to Nauvoo, and Dr. Foster remaining in Springfield to attend to an ailing Sidney Rigdon. *HC*, 4: 20–21.

17. Reminiscences of John Todd Stuart in *History of Sangamon County, Illinois* (Chicago: Inter-State Publishing Co., 1881), 197; Richard E. Hart, *Lincoln's Springfield: Seldom Visited Lincoln Sites* (Springfield, Ill.: Richard E. Hart, 2000), 7, 61.

18. Miers, *Lincoln Day-by-Day*, 119–20.

19. Lincoln to John Todd Stuart, March 1, 1840, *CW*, 1:206. Lincoln roomed with Joshua Speed during his first years in Springfield. The two men developed a close friendship that lasted Lincoln's lifetime. See chapter 2 in David Herbert Donald, *"We Are Lincoln Men": Abraham Lincoln and His Friends* (New York: Simon & Schuster, 2003).

20. Letter from John C. Bennett, July 27, 1840, Joseph Smith Papers website at http://josephsmithpapers.org/paperSummary/letter-from-john-c-bennett-27-july-1840, accessed October 17, 2014; see also *HC*, 4:169.

21. Lincoln, as one of the leaders of the Whig party in the state legislature, hoped to prevent a House vote that threatened the survival of the Illinois state bank. His attempt failed. Lincoln and two companions were lambasted in the newspapers for the unseemly spectacle of legislators scrambling out the window to thwart legislative business. See Miller, *Lincoln and His World*, 413–14; Michael Burlingame, *Abraham Lincoln: A Life* (Baltimore: John Hopkins University Press, 2008), 1:162–63; Harry E. Pratt, "Lincoln's 'Jump' from the Window," *Journal of the Illinois State Historical Society* 48:4 (Winter 1955), 458–61.

22. Sunderine (Wilson) Temple and Wayne C. Temple, *Illinois' Fifth Capitol: The House That Lincoln Built and Caused to Be Rebuilt—1837–1865* (Springfield, Ill.: Phillips Brothers Printers, 1988), 45.

23. *Journal of the House of Representatives of the Twelfth General Assembly of the State of Illinois* (Springfield, Ill.: W. Walters, Public Printer, 1840), 101, 110.

24. John C. Bennett to Joseph Smith, December 16, 1840, *HC*, 4: 248–49.

25. Regarding the controversy over the alleged Lincoln-Todd wedding engagement breakup, compare the following: chapter 8, "The Mary Todd 'Embrigglement,'" in Wilson, *Honor's Voice*, 233–64; Burlingame, *Abraham Lincoln*, 1:174–76, 181–82; and Baker, *Mary Todd Lincoln*, 83–90. Winkle provides a recent synthesis of the topic in *Abraham and Mary Lincoln*, 39–46.

26. Stakes are geographically based ecclesiastical administrative units in the Church of Jesus Christ of Latter-day Saints, somewhat analogous to a Catholic Church diocese.

27. *HC*, 4: 236. At the October 1840 General Conference in Nauvoo it had been decided, based on several applications, to organize stakes *"between this place and Kirtland [Ohio]." Ibid.*, 4:205. Hyrum Smith, Lyman Wight, and Almon W. Babbitt comprised the committee that implemented the Conference instructions by organizing stakes in the Illinois communities of Lima, Quincy, Columbus, Payson, Geneva, and Springfield, *Ibid.* 233, 236.

28. "The Church of 'the Latter Day Saints' . . . ," *Sangamo Journal,* May 14, 1841, 3:2.

29. These letters signed "Old Settler"—known as the "Sampson's Ghost Letters"—are attributed by some, but not all, historians to Abraham Lincoln. See Michael Burlingame, *The Inner World of Abraham Lincoln* (Urbana: University of Illinois Press, 1994), 211, note 38.

30. "First Reply to James Adams," September 6, 1837, *CW,* 1: 95–100; "Second Reply to James Adams," October 18, 1837, *Ibid.,* 101–6.

31. "An Old Settler," *Sangamo Journal,* October 6, 1837, 2:7.

32. Regarding the "Sampson's Ghost Letters," see Wilson, *Honor's Voice,* 174–79. More generally, see Wayne C. Temple, "James Adams and Abraham Lincoln," *Transactions of the Illinois Lodge of Research,* 16 (September 2007), 8–13; Kent L. Walgren, "James Adams: Early Springfield Mormon and Freemason," *Journal of the Illinois State Historical Society,* 75:2 (Summer 1982), 121–36. Presenting Adams in a more favorable light is Susan Easton Black, "James Adams of Springfield, Illinois: The Link between Abraham Lincoln and Joseph Smith," *Mormon Historical Studies* 10, no. 1 (Spring 2009), 33–49.

33. Regarding the evolution of Adams's relationship with Joseph Smith, see Walgren, "James Adams," and Black, "James Adams."

34. Glen M. Leonard, *Nauvoo: A Place of Peace, A People of Promise* (Salt Lake City, Utah: Desert Book Co. and BYU Press, 2002), 82.

35. For an explanation of plural marriage as instituted and practiced by Mormons in the mid-19th-century, see "Plural Marriage in Kirtland and Nauvoo," published on the official website of the LDS Church at https://www.lds.org/topics/plural-marriage-in-kirtland-and-nauvoo?lang=eng, accessed October 22, 2014.

36. Regarding the rekindled courtship between Abraham Lincoln and Mary Todd and their meetings in the Simeon Francis home, see Justin G. Turner and Linda Levitt Turner, *Mary Todd Lincoln: Her Life and Letters* (New York: Alfred A. Knopf, 1972), 29; Winkle, *Abraham and Mary Lincoln,* 44–45; Burlingame, *Abraham Lincoln,* 194; Wilson, *Honor's Voice,* 291.

37. Lincoln to Samuel D. Marshall, July 14, 1842, *CW,* 1: 290–91.

38. As one of the state's leading Whig politicians, Abraham Lincoln kept informed by reading newspapers from across Illinois. He would have been aware of the political war waged by Hancock County Whigs and others against Joseph Smith and the Mormons in the pages of Thomas Sharp's inflammatory newspaper, the *Warsaw Signal.* Receipts for "A. Lincoln" and "E[dward] D. Baker" (another prominent Springfield Whig) dated May 5, 1842, recording payment for two-year subscriptions to the *Warsaw Signal* are in the Warsaw Signal File, SC-1617, Manuscript Department, Abraham Lincoln Presidential Library, Springfield, Illinois.

39. Walgren, "James Adams," 133.

40. See Leonard, *Nauvoo,* 278–82.

41. Entry for Tuesday, December 13, 1842, recorded in the typed transcript of the Journal History of the Church of Jesus Christ of Latter-day Saints, LDS Church History Library, Salt Lake City, Utah. I'm indebted to Alex Smith, a member of the editorial staff of the Joseph Smith Papers, for verifying this citation for me. Others in the entourage with Hyrum Smith and Willard Richards were William Clayton, Henry G. Sherwood, Benjamin Covey, Peter Haws, Heber C. Kimball, Reynolds Cahoon, and Alpheus Cutler. An account of their Springfield trip (December 9–20, 1842) is recorded in Joseph Smith's journal by William Clayton and is found in Andrew Hedges, Alex D. Smith, and Richard Lloyd Anderson, eds., *Joseph Smith Papers—Journals,* volume 2,

December 1841–April 1843 (Salt Lake City, Utah: Church Historian's Press, 2011), 173–83 (hereinafter *JSJ*). See also *HC*, 5: 200–207.

42. An account of this Springfield trip (December 27, 1842–January 10, 1843) was recorded in Joseph Smith's journal by Willard Richards and is found in *JSJ*, 195–243. Those who accompanied Joseph Smith, besides Willard Richards, were Hyrum Smith, Wilson Law, John Taylor, Orson Hyde, William Marks, Levi Moffet, Peter Haws, Lorin Walker, Henry G. Sherwood, William Clayton, Edward Hunter, Theodore Turley, Dr. Harvey Tate, and Shadrach Roundy. See also *HC* 4: 209–47.

43. *JSJ*, 215. Joseph Smith apparently slept six of the eight nights he spent in Springfield (December 30 through January 6) on the couch in the home of James Adams. He slept in the home of William Sollar on the night of January 2 (*Ibid.*, 214), and in the home of Charles G. McGraw on the night of January 5 (*Ibid.*, 234).

44. Stephen T. Logan and Abraham Lincoln commenced their law partnership in 1841. Their office was in a building at what is now 108–110 North Fifth Street. The partners moved their office to the Tinsley Building sometime during the summer of 1843—several months *after* the Joseph Smith habeas corpus hearing in federal court. The last newspaper advertisement to list their original Fifth Street office address is dated June 15, 1843. The first newspaper advertisement to list their office as being in the Tinsley Building is dated August 31, 1843. See Mark Johnson, Marianna Munyer, and Richard Taylor, *The Lincoln-Herndon Law Offices Volunteer Manual* (Springfield, Ill.: Historic Sites Division of the Illinois Historic Preservation Agency, 1986), 62.

45. *JSJ*, 204, 225.

46. *Ibid.*, 204–5.

47. *Ibid.*, 206.

48. Harry E. Pratt, *Lincoln 1840–1846, Being the Day-by-Day Activities of Abraham Lincoln from January 1, 1840, to December 31, 1846* (Springfield, Ill.: Abraham Lincoln Association, 1939), 158; republished in Miers, *Lincoln Day-by-Day*, 198.

49. "Mind Your Steps Ladies," *Illinois State Register*, February 3, 1843, 3:7.

50. Irving Stone, *Love Is Eternal: A Novel of Mary Todd and Abraham Lincoln* (New York: Doubleday & Co., 1954), 138. Daniel Epstein writes that *"the press enthusiastically followed [Joseph Smith's] appearance at social functions at the American House"* but provides no citation to any such news reports. Epstein, *The Lincolns*, 60. Latter-day Saint authors writing for Latter-day Saint audiences today frequently include a New Year's Eve American House party appearance by Joseph Smith in their narratives. But they do not cite a source, or their cited sources do not check out. See, for example, Ron L. Andersen, *Abraham Lincoln and Joseph Smith: How Two Contemporaries Changed the Face of American History* (Springville, Utah: Plain Sight Publishing, 2014), 240.

51. *JSJ*, 206.

52. Regarding the worship services and sermons preached by Orson Hyde and John Taylor in the Old State Capitol's Hall of the Representatives, see *JSJ*, 206–9.

53. "The sun in all its splendor shines . . . ," *Quincy Whig*, January 11, 1843, 2:1.

54. A summary of the 1842–43 Missouri extradition attempt and transcriptions of the pertinent legal documents (including Judge Pope's decision) constitutes appendix 1 in *JSJ*, at 377–402. See also Andrew H. Hedges and Alex D. Smith, "Joseph Smith, John C. Bennett, and the Extradition Attempt, 1842," in Richard Neitzel Holzapfel and Kent P. Jackson, eds., *Joseph Smith the Prophet and Seer* (Provo, Utah: Religious Studies Center, Brigham Young University, 2010), 437–65.

55. *JSJ*, 211.

56. In a letter to his wife Lucretia at their home in Kaskaskia, Illinois, Judge Pope wrote of their daughter Cynthia being in attendance at the hearing: *"I did wish you were here yesterday when I delivered the opinion in the case of Smith (the Mormon Prophet). She [Cynthia] sat by my side, it would have made me most happy if you had been on the other side."* Quoted in Paul M. Angle, "Nathaniel Pope, 1784–1850: A Memoir," *Illinois State Historical Society Transactions for the Year 1936*, no. 43 (Springfield, Ill.: Illinois State Historical Library, 1936), 111–81, at 165.

57. The unusually large number of women in attendance at Joseph Smith's hearing provoked ridicule in one Quincy, Illinois, newspaper and drew a spirited response in another. Quincy correspondent "Alpha" (reportedly Isaac N. Morris) cleverly employed widely recognized negative inferences to impugn any sentiments of tolerance or sympathy for the Mormons. Alpha was quoted as writing,

> *During Smith's trial Judge Pope sat upon the bench with three ladies upon each side of him. The smile of those associate judges added very much to the solemnity of the proceedings. It is said that they were there that the Prophet might cast upon them the "blessing of Jacob." Their attendance, however, was a compliment, I suppose, paid to the virtue of the Holy Prophet. And as they gazed upon his manly form, probably the power of imagination brought around them the fancied scenery of Nauvoo—there was the Temple—there was the Prophet's palace—there was Jo and his Mormon virgins, of which rumor, with her thousand tongues, has said so much. . . . With such a field for the imagination, how could the ladies resist sympathizing with the Prophet, and attending his trial. They are surely excusable.*

Rising to the defense of the insulted ladies whom Alpha had implied were present at the hearing not *"from any virtuous impulse,"* the incensed editors of the *Quincy Whig* decried the insinuating report as *"unmanly,"* a specimen of *"indecency,"* and *"a base libel upon the Court."* "'Alpha'—I. N. Morris," *Quincy Whig*, March 1, 1843, 2:3.

58. Isaac N. Arnold, *Reminiscences of the Illinois Bar Forty Years Ago: Lincoln and Douglas as Orators and Lawyers by Hon. Isaac N. Arnold, Read Before "The Bar Association of the State of Illinois," Springfield, January 7, 1881* (Chicago, Ill.: Fergus Printing Company, 1881), 6.

59. *Ibid.*, 7.

60. See Bryon C. Andreasen, *Defending Judge Browne: A Case Study in the Legal, Legislative, and Political Workings of Abraham Lincoln's Illinois* (Springfield, Ill.: Illinois Supreme Court Historic Commission, 2013). It might be more likely that Lincoln was in the state capitol building observing the final phases of Judge Browne's removal hearing. Lincoln had participated in the early phase of the hearing but had been dismissed along with several other attorneys during the course of the proceedings.

61. *HC*, 5: 245.

62. *JSJ*, 235–36.

63. See Andreasen, *Defending Judge Browne*, appendix 2, "Did the Mormon Prophet Joseph Smith Attend Judge Browne's Address Hearing?," 83–93.

64. Miers, *Lincoln Day-by-Day*, 231–32.

65. Speech at Springfield, Illinois, June 26, 1857, *CW*, 2:398–410, at 399. See, generally, John Y. Simon, "Lincoln, Douglas, and Popular Sovereignty: The Mormon Dimension," in John Y. Simon, Harold Holzer, and Dawn Vogel, eds., *Lincoln Revisited: New Insights from the Lincoln*

Forum (New York: Fordham University Press, 2007), 45–56; George U. Hubbard, "Abraham Lincoln as Seen by the Mormons," *Utah Historical Quarterly* 31:2 (Spring 1963), 91–108, at 95–97. Regarding Douglas's long and shifting relationship with the Mormons, see Bruce A. Van Orden, "Stephen A. Douglas and the Mormons," in H. Dean Garrett, ed., *Regional Studies in Latter-day Saint History: Illinois* (Provo, Utah: Brigham Young University, Department of Church History and Doctrine, 1995), 359–78.

66. Richard D. Poll, "The Mormon Question, 1850-1865: A Study in Politics and Public Opinion" (Ph.D. diss., University of California, Berkeley, 1948), 274.

67. Thomas Ford, *A History of Illinois: From Its Commencement as a State in 1818 to 1847* (1854; repr., Urbana: Ill.: University of Illinois Press, 1995), 249.

68. Since post–Civil War times, Latter-day Saints have revered Lincoln as an instrument in God's hands for the furtherance of divine purposes, without necessarily ascribing to Lincoln an understanding or consciousness of Mormon doctrine or beliefs. But recently some LDS writers have argued that Lincoln had close association with Latter-day Saints in Illinois (see Anderson, *Abraham Lincoln and Joseph Smith*) and that Lincoln's alleged close reading of the *Book of Mormon* inspired his understanding of the Civil War and influenced his views on emancipation (see Timothy Ballard, *The Lincoln Hypothesis: A Modern-Day Abolitionist Investigates the Possible Connection between Joseph Smith, the* Book of Mormon*, and Abraham Lincoln* [Salt Lake City: Deseret Book, 2014]). Working from an LDS interpretive framework of providential history, these authors tend to overestimate Lincoln's relationship with Mormons and overreach the evidence. They give more interpretive weight to fragmentary, ambiguous sources (often hearsay) than these sources can bear. A desire to align Lincoln with a faith tradition is certainly not unique to Latter-day Saints. Christians in general have always sought to assure themselves that Lincoln was one of them. Numerous Christian denominations have laid claim to a special relationship with him. Several even claim to have baptized him. Indeed, the literature on Lincoln and religion is immense. Much of it suffers from similar analytical shortcomings. Some recent works include Ferenc Morton Szasz, *Lincoln and Religion* (Carbondale: Southern Illinois University Press, 2014); Stephen Mansfield, *Lincoln's Battle with God: A President's Struggle with Faith and What It Meant for America* (Nashville: Thomas Nelson, 2012); Samuel W. Morel and Lucas E. Morel, "Abraham Lincoln's Religion: The Case for His Ultimate Belief in a Personal, Sovereign God," *Journal of the Abraham Lincoln Association* 33, no. 1 (Winter 2012), 38–74.

69. Robert Remini, *Joseph Smith* (New York: Viking Penguin, 2002), 180.

70. Harold Bloom, *The American Religion: The Emergence of the Post-Christian Nation* (New York: Simon & Schuster, 1992), 104, 96–97.

71. Karen Lynn Davidson, David J. Whittaker, Mark Ashurst-McGee, Richard L. Jensen, eds., *The Joseph Smith Papers—Histories*, volume 1, *Joseph Smith Histories, 1832–1844* (Salt Lake City, Utah: Church Historian's Press, 2012), 222–23. (Joseph Smith—History 1:33). Also, *HC* 1: 11–2.

PART 1. NAUVOO

Map of Nauvoo, Illinois, identifying story locations with corresponding story numbers.

Story Site Locations

1. Lincoln and Nauvoo
2. Unsuccessful Peacemaker
3. Nauvoo and Lincoln's Whig Rivals
4. Abraham Jonas, Whig Politician
5. The Battle of Nauvoo
6. Mormon Emissary to Lincoln
7. Daniel Wells, Nauvoo Whig
8. Stephen A. Douglas and Nauvoo
9. Lincoln and Joseph Smith III
10. The President and the Apostle
11. Lincoln and the Gunsmith

1. LINCOLN AND NAUVOO

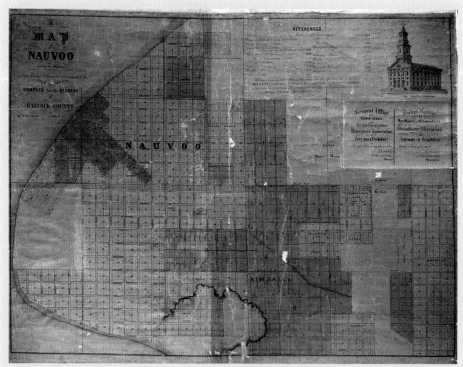

This map of Nauvoo, compiled from Hancock County records by A. Cherill in about 1846, reflects the city as the people of Abraham Lincoln's day would have known it. The English and German advertisements in the margin indicate that the map may have been used to promote immigration in the wake of the Mormon exodus.

ABRAHAM LINCOLN HAD THE CAPACITY TO CONJURE IN HIS

mind's eye the beauty and potential of Nauvoo through maps and descriptions (he was a former surveyor), even though he apparently never viewed its panoramic vista in person. As a member of the Illinois House of Representatives he voted with the majority to pass a charter that incorporated Nauvoo as a city, signed by Governor Thomas Carlin on December 16, 1840. Initially the charter was not controversial, it being similar in most respects to charters granted to other Illinois cities. Eventually it became a point of contention, however. Opponents perceived in the charter a worrisome concentration of legislative, executive, and judicial powers in the hands of a few—while Joseph Smith and others interpreted the charter in ways they believed necessary to protect the community from the kinds of abuses Mormons had suffered in other locations. The Illinois legislature revoked the Nauvoo charter seven months after Joseph Smith's death. Lincoln played no part in revoking the charter, his last legislative term having expired before the controversy erupted.

James H. Ralston.

SOME 200 NAUVOO VOTERS

scratched Lincoln's name from their ballots during the November 1840 presidential election. Lincoln was one of the electors for Whig candidate William Henry Harrison—whom most Mormons supported. But to demonstrate a degree of political even-handedness and to express gratitude for bipartisan sympathy received on their arrival in Illinois, Mormon voters wrote in the name of Quincy Democrat James H. Ralston in place of Lincoln (whose name was listed last on the Whig ticket). Lincoln apparently took no offense. Nauvoo's lobbyist in Springfield, John C. Bennett, reported, *"Lincoln, whose name we erased from the electoral ticket in November had the magnanimity to vote for [the Nauvoo charter], and came forward, after the final vote to the bar of the house, and cordially congratulated me on its passage."*

Election on the 2d of November.
FOR PRESIDENT
MARTIN VAN BUREN.
FOR VICE PRESIDENT
RICHARD M. JOHNSON.
FOR ELECTORS OF PRESIDENT AND VICE PRESIDENT
ADAM W. SNYDER, of St. Clair,
ISAAC P. WALKER, of Vermillion,
JOHN W. ELDREDGE of Cook,
JOHN A. McCLERNAND, of Gallatin,
JAMES H. RALSTON, of Adams

Abraham Lincoln in 1846 (earliest known photograph).

FOR PRESIDENT,
WM. HENRY HARRISON, OF OHIO.
FOR VICE-PRESIDENT,
JOHN TYLER, OF VIRGINIA.

CANDIDATES FOR PRESIDENTIAL ELECTORS.
CYRUS WALKER, OF M'DONOUGH,
BUCKNER S. MORRIS, OF COOK,
SAMUEL D. MARSHALL, OF GALLATIN,
EDWIN B. WEBB, OF WHITE,
ABRAM LINCOLN, OF SANGAMON.

2. UNSUCCESSFUL PEACEMAKER

The temple tower was the vantage point from which Quincy mayor John Wood watched the fighting unfold ten blocks to the east on the outskirts of the city during the Battle of Nauvoo on September 12, 1846. Before Nauvoo's defenders surrendered to the attacking militia, Mayor Wood left for Quincy saddened that he had failed in his mission to avert bloodshed. He experienced a similar scenario 15 years later as a delegate to a national peace conference that failed to avert the American Civil War.

MAYOR JOHN WOOD OF

Quincy, Illinois, was considered fair-minded by both Mormons and non-Mormons. So when trouble erupted in Hancock County in September 1846 (after Brigham Young and most Mormons had evacuated Nauvoo) it was natural that Illinois governor Thomas Ford turned to Wood for assistance. Anti-Mormon extremists were determined to storm Nauvoo and force the remaining Mormons out. The governor asked Wood to negotiate a truce. Wood tried twice to persuade the unauthorized militia to obey state orders to disband. Extremist militiamen rebuffed him and attacked the city. Nauvoo's defenders slowly gave ground in house-to-house fighting. At least four persons died. To avert further bloodshed the citizens of Nauvoo surrendered several days later on assurances that no one else would be hurt as long as the remaining Mormons left immediately. Church trustees surrendered the temple keys to Quincy negotiators. Then the anti-Mormons occupied Nauvoo. In defiance of the agreement, the militia forced many new non-Mormon citizens, as well as Mormons, to leave. Arsonists burned the temple two years later.

ABRAHAM LINCOLN WAS LARGELY

responsible for John Wood's nomination as lieutenant governor in 1856. In the decades following the Battle of Navuoo, Wood—like Lincoln—followed his antislavery sentiments into the fledgling Republican Party. Wood was elected. Then when Governor William H. Bissell died in office early in 1860, Wood served out the remainder of his term as governor. Wood permitted Lincoln to use the governor's office in the State Capitol building in Springfield as a temporary headquarters for the president-elect. In February 1861 Wood joined other delegates from around the country at a national convention in Washington, D.C., to make one last desperate attempt to avoid civil war. He served as Illinois' quartermaster general and later, at the age of sixty-four, as a colonel of an Illinois volunteer regiment during the Civil War.

John Wood was mayor of Quincy, Illinois, in 1846 when the Mormons were expelled from the state, and served as the governor of Illinois at the time Lincoln was elected president in 1860.

3. NAUVOO AND LINCOLN'S WHIG RIVALS

John J. Hardin.

BOTH OF ABRAHAM LINCOLN'S

chief rivals in Illinois' Whig party performed military duties at Nauvoo. When anti-Mormons began intimidating local county officials after the August 1844 elections, Governor Thomas Ford appointed General John J. Hardin of Jacksonville and Colonel Edward D. Baker of Springfield to command the state troops that accompanied the governor here in September. Ford aimed to preserve order and to assist in capturing the accused murderers of Joseph and Hyrum Smith. Colonel Baker, however, on his own initiative crossed the Mississippi River and negotiated the surrender of several fugitives on terms favorable to the accused—an insubordinate act that undercut the governor. Ford was mercilessly ridiculed for what appeared to have been an unnecessary military expedition. A year later Ford ordered General Hardin to return here to

Edward D. Baker.

Governor Thomas Ford and state militiamen led by General John J. Hardin and Colonel Edward D. Baker inspected the Temple when they arrived in Nauvoo in September 1844. "[T]hey appeared astonished, but were civil," Mormons reported. Hardin returned with troops the next September (1845) and rested them on the parade grounds directly northeast of the Temple. By then the nearly completed Temple would have looked even more impressive than it had the year before. Ford gave Hardin authority to command the Nauvoo Legion, but Hardin never exercised it.

restore order following an outbreak of house burnings against the Mormons in September 1845. Hardin imposed martial law in the county during negotiations that resulted in Brigham Young agreeing that the Mormons would leave Illinois the next spring.

LINCOLN DIDN'T ASPIRE TO MILITARY GLORY LIKE HIS WHIG RIVALS

Hardin and Baker. They all lived in the Seventh Congressional District (Nauvoo was in the Sixth)—the only district where Whigs were consistently competitive. They allowed each other to take a turn in Congress: Hardin took office in 1843, Baker in 1845, and Lincoln in 1847, though Hardin, a cousin of Mary Lincoln and Lincoln's chief rival, did so reluctantly. Previously Hardin had intervened to help prevent a saber duel involving Lincoln, and he helped in reconciling the Lincolns after their broken engagement. The Lincolns felt closer to Baker, however, even naming their second son after him. All three men met violent deaths: Hardin at the Battle of Buena Vista in the Mexican-American War, Baker at the Battle of Ball's Bluff in the Civil War, and Lincoln by assassination.

Abraham Lincoln served as a captain in the state militia during Illinois' Black Hawk War (1832), but that was the extent of his military experience—until he became commander-in-chief of U.S. forces during the Civil War.

4. ABRAHAM JONAS, WHIG POLITICIAN

NAUVOO EXPOSITOR.

—THE TRUTH, THE WHOLE TRUTH, AND NOTHING BUT THE TRUTH.—

VOL. 1.]　　　　　　NAUVOO, ILLINOIS, FRIDAY, JUNE 7, 1844.　　　　　[NO. 1.

MORMONS VOTED IN LARGE

numbers for Abraham Jonas from neighboring Adams County in the August 1842 state elections—helping him win a seat in the state House of Representatives and sending him to Springfield, where he solidified his friendship with fellow Whig party member Abraham Lincoln. It was Jonas who, as Illinois' Masonic grand master, had cleared the way for a

The building where the Expositor *newspaper was published as it appeared in 1915, before it was razed.*

Abraham Jonas and other Whigs in western Illinois began supporting local anti-Mormons when it became evident that the Mormon vote couldn't be guaranteed for the Whigs. Jonas secretly supplied Mormon dissidents in Nauvoo with a printing press to publish their newspaper—the Nauvoo Expositor. *Nauvoo officials ordered the* Expositor *press destroyed as a public nuisance. That order—acted on at the* Expositor's *office on Mulholland Street in June 1844—started a chain of events that ended in Joseph Smith's murder three weeks later.*

Masonic lodge in Nauvoo, and who presided at public installation ceremonies for the lodge, held in the grove below the temple construction site in March 1842. Fellow Masons in Quincy and other areas of Illinois resented what they perceived to be Jonas's favoritism toward the Mormons and murmured that he was cynically using his privileges as grand master to court Mormon political support for his personal advancement. Later, when anti-Mormons in the area charged the Nauvoo lodge with irregularities, Jonas unsuccessfully defended the Mormon Masons before the Illinois Grand Lodge. Shifting political winds, however, eventually caused Jonas to turn against the Mormons.

Abraham Jonas.

"DOUGLASITES WOULD AS SOON SEE OLD NICK HERE AS YOURSELF,"

Jonas wrote Abraham Lincoln when inviting him to speak against Stephen Douglas at an 1854 anti-Kansas-Nebraska Act rally in Quincy. As Illinois' Whig Party gradually disintegrated over slavery, many former Whigs joined the American Party—an anti-Catholic, anti-immigrant organization commonly called the "Know-Nothings." Lincoln did not share that party's nativist attitudes, but he was nevertheless accused by local Democrats of entering a Quincy "Know-Nothing" lodge during his 1854 visit. To squelch the hurtful rumors, Lincoln secretly wrote to Jonas, asking him to have some Know-Nothings sign affidavits swearing Lincoln never attended the lodge. It was Jonas who persuaded Lincoln to make his first foray into Hancock County during the 1858 Senate campaign against Douglas by speaking at a nominating convention in Augusta.

Panorama mural painted by Mormon artist C. C. A. Christensen sometime after 1878.

Late in the summer of 1846 anti-Mormon extremists planned attacks to force expulsion of Nauvoo's few remaining Mormons. New non-Mormon settlers who had purchased cheap Mormon property in the city joined Mormons under Governor Ford's military emissary Major Benjamin Clifford to set up defenses along Winchester Street. On September 12, 1846, cannon fire erupted along this line, followed by house fighting in this vicinity. The battle lasted two hours—until both sides ran out of ammunition. Nauvoo's defenders surrendered several days later.

ABRAHAM LINCOLN WAS SEVERAL COUNTIES AWAY

attending court at Tremont when an army of anti-Mormon extremists besieged Nauvoo. Their initial commander was James W. Singleton, a Whig lawyer and aspiring politician from Brown County. Singleton's objective had been to enforce an arrest warrant. But when he realized that the warrant was merely a pretext for attacking Nauvoo, he sought a peaceful resolution. His militiamen refused. They also refused to obey state officials sent by Governor Thomas Ford to prevent violence. Singleton resigned command rather than be party to an unauthorized attack on civilians. Two years previous to what became known as the Battle of Nauvoo, Singleton commanded state troops that accompanied Governor Ford to Nauvoo, where Ford spoke at the very moment Joseph and Hyrum Smith were murdered in Carthage, Illinois, in 1844. The following year—1845—Singleton played an important role at a regional meeting in Carthage that demanded all Latter-day Saints leave Illinois.

JAMES W. SINGLETON BEGAN HIS

political career as a Lincoln ally. In the years after the "Mormon War," however, the two men drifted apart. When the Whig Party disintegrated in the mid-1850s Singleton became a Democrat rather than follow Lincoln into the antislavery Republican Party. During the Civil War Singleton was a prominent "Copperhead"—a severe critic of Lincoln, emancipation, and the war. Lincoln told his secretary John Hay that Singleton was *a miracle of meanness."* Nevertheless, near the end of the war Lincoln permitted Singleton to engage in speculative cotton and tobacco trading across enemy lines. Singleton reported performing a peace mission for Lincoln by meeting with Confederate leaders in Richmond. He claimed that Lincoln was willing to make peace without insisting on the abolition of slavery—unfairly casting a shadow on the President's reputation.

James W. Singleton caused problems for Mormons during the 1840s, and for Abraham Lincoln during the 1850s and 1860s.

6. MORMON EMISSARY TO LINCOLN

ABRAHAM LINCOLN MET WITH DR. JOHN M. BERNHISEL MORE

frequently than with probably any other Latter-day Saint. As Utah's territorial delegate to Congress, Bernhisel conferred with Lincoln at least eight times from December 1861 to March 1863. Potential Utah statehood and choices for territorial officials were chief topics of discussion. Bernhisel was surprised the first time he visited Lincoln when the president called him in ahead of others who were waiting in line. He described Lincoln as *"affable and agreeable,"* considering him the warmest natured of the five American presidents he dealt with during his ten years of Congressional service. But Lincoln was coy when it came to disappointing those who petitioned him, using humor and indirection to deflect contention—causing Bernhisel to erroneously conclude, *"The President appears to take matters and things very easy; neither the war nor anything else seems to trouble him."* Indicative was Lincoln's excuse to Bernhisel for having appointed an incompetent Utah official. Just as *"Adam . . . rolled the blame [for transgression] on Eve and upon the devil,"* he, too, blamed the devil for the failed appointment.

JUST AS BERNHISEL WAS BRIGHAM

Young's emissary to President Lincoln, he had also been Joseph Smith's emissary to Illinois governor Thomas Ford, representing the Prophet in correspondence and meetings with the governor in events prior to the martyrdom. Afterward, Dr. Bernhisel helped Emma Smith

Dr. John M. Bernhisel had a thriving New York City medical practice when he converted to the Mormon faith. In April 1843 he moved to Nauvoo intending to practice medicine. He planned to build a house on a lot south of the James and White Streets intersection (James Street no longer exists). But Joseph Smith asked him to join his household at the recently completed Mansion House, instead. The urbane, scholarly doctor became Joseph Smith's personal attaché during the last year of the Prophet's life.

tend to her fitful newborn son, David Hyrum Smith. A boarder recorded, *"Doctor Burnhisel and Emma, together, by medicine and management finally overcame"* the child's colic. Though Emma's family didn't follow the Saints to Utah, Bernhisel nevertheless had cordial relations with Emma and maintained a life-long interest in David Hyrum.

The federal government's relationship with Utah was of paramount concern to Dr. Bernhisel. But for Lincoln, it was just one of the many problems he faced as president.

Emma Smith with her baby, David Hyrum Smith, who was born almost five months after his father was killed. Courtesy Community of Christ.

Lincoln wrote this note of introduction to Secretary of War Edwin M. Stanton relaying Dr. Bernhisel's request that federal troops garrisoned in Salt Lake City be moved elsewhere for better use. The troops remained, however.

Daniel Wells and Abraham Lincoln were both young men when their paths crossed in Carthage. Wells served on a jury for a murder case that Lincoln was trying. Politically, they were both Whigs. "Squire Wells" served as constable, justice of the peace, and militia officer. He befriended the Mormons and provided land for the temple. Intrigued by Joseph Smith's doctrine of salvation for the dead, he joined the Church when the last Mormons were forced to leave. In Utah he became a counselor to Church president Brigham Young.

MUSKET BALLS WHIZZED

about the farm of Daniel Wells during the Battle of Nauvoo in September 1846. Wells served as a military aide to Major Benjamin Clifford, who Illinois governor Thomas Ford appointed as commander of the forces defending Nauvoo. During the battle, Wells mounted a horse and exposed himself to enemy fire while rallying a company of men to come to the aid of those bearing the brunt of the attack. When Nauvoo's defenders later surrendered, Wells—one of the "old settlers" from the pre-Mormon period—was forced to leave Nauvoo with the rest of the Mormons. Wells later said that as he crossed the Mississippi River to leave, mocking enemy militiamen fired their cannon at him. Somehow he retrieved one of the cannon balls. He sent it to Governor Ford as a reminder of the state's failure to enforce the rule of law against the renegade anti-Mormon militias. In Utah, Wells became the commander of the Nauvoo Legion.

Daniel Wells's Nauvoo farmhouse in a dilapidated state.

THE STORY IS TOLD THAT ON

meeting Daniel Wells for the first time Abraham Lincoln reportedly exclaimed, *"Prepare to die! I swore that if I ever met a man who was uglier than I am I would shoot him."* To which Wells replied, *"Shoot away. If I am as ugly as you are, then I don't want to live."* This humorous Lincoln anecdote is not unique to Daniel Wells. Over the decades many other people "remembered" versions of the story involving other people at other places. Lincoln is known to have repeated jokes and stories, so it is possible that Wells was one of many who heard some version of it from Lincoln. The Wells version can be traced back to the early part of the 20th century, when Church president Heber J. Grant enjoyed telling the story.

Heber J. Grant, LDS Church president from 1918 to 1945, enjoyed telling Wells's Lincoln story.

8. STEPHEN A. DOUGLAS AND NAUVOO

CRITICS OF STEPHEN A. DOUGLAS ACCUSED HIM OF PANDERING

to Mormons for political purposes. As Illinois secretary of state he supported the Nauvoo charter; as a judge he issued favorable court rulings for Joseph Smith; as a congressman he helped negotiate the Saints' exodus from Nauvoo and provided them assistance in their journey west. The Prophet had once declared Douglas a *"master spirit"* and a friend of the Saints. He is also supposed to have warned Douglas:

> *Judge, you will aspire to the presidency of the United States; and if you ever turn your hand against me or the Latter-day Saints, you will feel*

Joseph Mustering the Nauvoo Legion, *by 19th-century Mormon artist C. C. A. Christensen.*

Stephen A. Douglas was an observer on May 7, 1842, when the Nauvoo Legion held a massive sham battle on parade grounds east of town. Judge Douglas had been holding circuit court in Carthage when he received word of the Legion's planned exercises. He promptly adjourned court and hurried to Nauvoo to witness the spectacle. Later that day, Joseph Smith invited Douglas and other visiting dignitaries to join the Legion's staff officers and their ladies at his home for a "sumptuous dinner."

the weight of the hand of the Almighty upon you; and you will live to see and know that I have testified the truth to you; for the conversation of this day will stick to you through life.

Douglas ultimately did turn against the Saints, deriding them at the time of the "Utah War" in 1857 as a *"pestiferous, disgusting cancer."* He never succeeded in his quest for the presidency.

LINCOLN REFUSED TO ATTACK HIS

arch foe Stephen Douglas on the "Mormon question" during their intense 1858 Illinois senatorial campaign, even though Douglas was vulnerable on the issue. Douglas had staked his political career on the principle of "popular sovereignty"— that people should be free to decide on the *local* level such questions as whether to permit slavery. Both before and after the 1858 campaign, Lincoln publicly noted the inconsistency in Douglas's position—that if Douglas would permit people to vote their moral conscience to allow slavery in the territories, why shouldn't he allow Mormons to vote their moral conscience to allow polygamy in the Utah Territory? Though colleagues encouraged Lincoln to stigmatize Douglas with "Mormonism," Lincoln chose to ignore political expediency and left the Mormons out of his rhetorical attacks on Douglas—focusing instead on slavery.

Douglas in the 1840s when he was the Saints' friend.

Douglas in the late-1850s when he was the Saints' foe.

9. LINCOLN AND JOSEPH SMITH III

Joseph Smith III (about 1860), oldest son of Mormonism's founder, Joseph Smith Jr., had favored Stephen Douglas—until he attended an 1858 Douglas rally in Carthage. He reported that Douglas "showed unmistakable signs of intoxication," *was* "unsteady on his feet," *and his* "tongue [was] so thick" *that his words were incomprehensible. Finally friends interceded and sat Douglas down, explaining that the Senator was* "suddenly indisposed." "So away went Mr. Douglas," *Joseph Smith III recalled,* "and away went my prejudices in his favor." Courtesy Community of Christ.

JOSEPH SMITH III WAS AN

eyewitness to Abraham Lincoln's campaign speech at Carthage during his 1858 senatorial campaign against Stephen Douglas. Years later Joseph remembered that Lincoln *"looked so inferior to what I had in mind . . . [his] appearance was anything but prepossessing or reassuring."* To Joseph, Lincoln's *"eyes were dull, his manner awkward, and his voice sharp. . . . I felt very sorry for him."* Lincoln spoke from a platform over which a canopy of leafy branches had been erected to shield the speaker from the sun. But when Lincoln squared his shoulders and straightened up, his head hit the branches! *"A humorous expression crossed his face and, turning his head slightly to one side, with a sudden movement he thrust it upward, entirely through that bowery business above him! There he stood towering, like some queer creature, whose head was detached from its body!"* The crowd roared with approval and Lincoln went on to spellbind his audience. *"By the time the lecture was over, I was completely and altogether a Lincoln man,"* Joseph recalled.

GOVERNOR THOMAS FORD

addressed Nauvoo's citizens from a platform across the street from the Mansion House at about the same time that Joseph and Hyrum Smith were murdered in

Carthage. He warned Mormons of the *"hatred and prejudice"* against them. Ford later had strong words for Abraham Lincoln, identifying him as one of the petty politicians responsible for *"much calamity"* caused by excessive state spending. Joseph Smith III didn't share Ford's low opinion of Lincoln, whose antislavery views he admired. In April 1860, while Lincoln was running for the presidency, Joseph was ordained prophet of the Reorganized Church of Jesus Christ of Latter Day Saints (today known as the Community of Christ). Lincoln left no record regarding the Reorganization movement. U.S. presidents Grant, Hayes, and Garfield each ignored suggestions that Joseph Smith III be appointed Utah territorial governor.

Governor Thomas Ford spoke across the street from Joseph Smith's home in Nauvoo while a mob was attacking Joseph Smith in the Carthage jail.

Joseph Smith's Mansion House is today a historic site run by the Community of Christ church. Courtesy Community of Christ.

10. THE PRESIDENT AND THE APOSTLE

George Q. Cannon was age 34 when he visited Lincoln in the White House in 1862. Nineteen years earlier he had arrived in Nauvoo as a teenager. His family lived directly across the street from his uncle, Apostle John Taylor. For lack of room in his father's house, young George lived with the Taylors. He became a printer's apprentice to his uncle, working on the Times & Seasons *and other Church publications.*

The president during the early months of the war as Cannon would have seen him.

PRESIDENT LINCOLN WAS

anxiously awaiting war news regarding the movements of Confederate general "Stonewall" Jackson in the Shenandoah Valley, when Mormon apostle George Q. Cannon and two companions called on him at the White House on June 9, 1862. Lincoln surprisingly took time to meet with them. Cannon had been ordained an apostle two years earlier and had been serving as the Church's mission president in Great Britain when unbeknownst to him he was elected senator as part of an effort by Utah's residents to obtain statehood. Senator-elect Cannon's presidential visit was part of an attempt to persuade Congress to accept Utah as a state. *"[Lincoln] received us very kindly and without formality,"* Cannon recorded. *"The President has a plain, but shrewd and rather pleasant face. . . . He looks much better than I expected . . . from my knowledge of the cares and labors of his position, and is quite humorous, scarcely permitting a visit to pass without uttering some joke."* Lincoln was tactfully noncommittal about Utah statehood. Congress ultimately denied the petition and Utah remained a territory.

The Executive Mansion in Civil War times.

GEORGE Q. CANNON'S FATHER WAS

standing at the front gate of his home when he heard the news of the assassinations of Joseph and Hyrum Smith. It fell to him, an accomplished cabinetmaker, to construct their coffins. Young George stood beside the bodies of the murdered brothers as his father made the plaster casts from which he created death masks. *"A lock of the Prophet's hair was caught in the plaster mask, and I remember father taking some scissors and clipping the hair and then giving me the scissors to hold while he went on with his work,"* George later recalled. As an apostle and counselor to Church presidents, Cannon met more American presidents than just Abraham Lincoln—eventually having face-to-face meetings with presidents Grant, Hayes, Garfield, Cleveland, and McKinley.

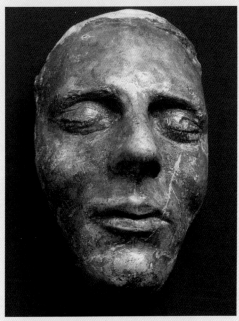

Joseph Smith's death mask.

11. LINCOLN AND THE GUNSMITH

"TWO FRONTIERSMEN YARNING!"

Jonathan Browning and his wife, Elizabeth.

Orville Hickman Browning—the gunsmith's cousin; Lincoln's friend and associate.

That was how Jonathan Browning described his meeting with Abraham Lincoln. They shared frontier southern backgrounds, were about the same height, were near the same age, and—according to Browning—shared a penchant for homespun humor. Browning claimed that Lincoln visited his home in Quincy, Illinois, and the two started swapping stories. Lincoln laughed heartily on learning that the gunsmith had once traded a gun for a Bible. It was like *"turning swords into plowshares,"* Lincoln quipped, in reference to Isaiah's Biblical admonition. Browning then confessed that the traded gun had been defective, having a mainspring that was *"pretty weak."* In mock indignation Lincoln declared, *"You cheated in a trade for a Bible!"* *"Not exactly,"* Browning retorted. *"When I got looking through that Bible at home, I found about half the New Testament was missing!"* The convulsive

Jonathan Browning moved his family from Tennessee to the growing Mississippi River town of Quincy, Illinois, in 1834. Also living in Quincy was Browning's Kentucky cousin, Orville Hickman Browning, an associate of Abraham Lincoln's who, according to family lore, introduced the future president to his gunsmith cousin. Jonathan was among those who befriended Mormon refugees fleeing Missouri in 1838–39. He read the Book of Mormon *and converted to the Mormon faith, moving to Nauvoo in 1842.*

In Nauvoo, Browning made five-shot slide rifles like this one.

laughter of the two men *"near to shook the logs"* of the cabin. At least that's how Browning told the story to his family many years later, after Lincoln had become famous.

HAD BROWNING NOT BEEN FAR

away in frontier Utah during the American Civil War, he may have had the chance to consult with Lincoln regarding firearms for the Union army. In the 1840s Browning manufactured slide guns and cylinder repeating rifles for use by Mormon pioneers, both being among the earliest repeating rifle models invented in America. Two decades later, President Lincoln took a special interest in repeating rifles for Union soldiers. He met many inventors and test-fired weapons at the Treasury Park near the White House. Displaying his own inventiveness, Lincoln whittled an improved gun sight from a stick of pine for a Spencer carbine he was testing—and then placed 12 of 14 rapidly fired shots directly on target. Browning would have certainly appreciated the president's ingenuity even more than his marksmanship.

Lincoln testing a repeating rifle.

An actual target used by President Lincoln in wartime Washington showing his marksmanship, displayed at the Illinois State Military Museum in Springfield, Illinois.

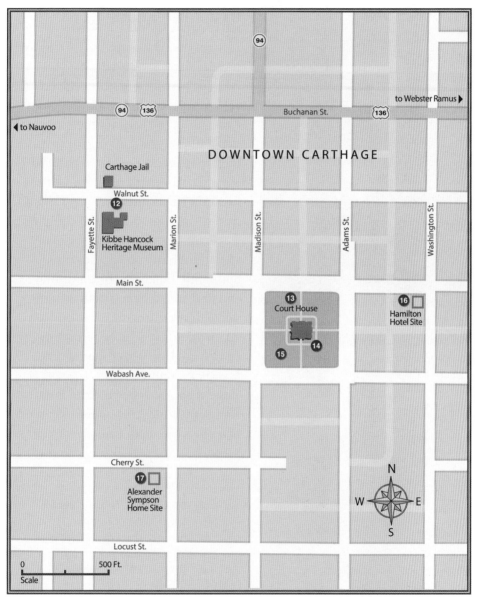

Map of Carthage, Illinois, identifying story locations with corresponding story numbers.

Story Site Locations
12. Hancock County's Lincoln
13. Lincoln's Failed Murder Case
14. Lincoln's Carthage Speech
15. Lincoln's Agricultural World
16. Hamilton House
17. Lincoln's "Confidential Friend"

12. HANCOCK COUNTY'S LINCOLN

Stephen A. Douglas's long association with Hancock County gave him a political advantage over Lincoln in 1858 and 1860.

HANCOCK COUNTY WAS

Douglas country. Stephen A. Douglas traveled here many times when he presided over the district circuit court at Carthage. He later won election to Congress in the neighboring congressional district. And during his years in the U.S. Senate he achieved national fame. Local voters knew him well and by the late 1850s usually voted Democratic. Much less familiar to them was Abraham Lincoln. Hancock County was off his beaten track. Lincoln's Springfield home was 115 miles away and in different judicial and congressional districts, and he never held a statewide office. Still, he vigorously carried the U.S. Senate contest into Hancock County in 1858. The vote was closer than usual, but Lincoln lost. In later years, Lincoln's opponents carried majorities here both times he ran for president—voters favoring Douglas in

According to a Chicago Tribune *article published in 1893, Lincoln had this picture taken in Carthage by an itinerant photographer at the insistence of his friend Alexander Sympson while Lincoln was campaigning in October 1858. But most experts agree it was taken by T. P. Pearson at his shop in Macomb, Illinois, in August 1858. Either way, the image reflects how Lincoln appeared to Hancock County residents during Illinois' 1858 Senate contest.*

1860 and General George B. McClellan in 1864. Lincoln just couldn't win Hancock County.

LINCOLN HAD MANY STRONG

supporters in Hancock County, despite being outnumbered. Attesting to this are a variety of rare campaign artifacts exhibited in the Kibbe Hancock Heritage Museum in Carthage. These artifacts also document the importance of political pageantry in the lives of 19th-century Americans, including the Latter-day Saints, who dominated politics in the county in the early 1840s. Carthage was less developed then. There was an unobstructed view between the courthouse square and the new jail that was completed in 1841—the jail in which Joseph Smith was murdered three years later. Today the Carthage Jail is a historic site run by the Church of Jesus Christ of Latter-day Saints. The Kibbe Museum is across the street, directly south of the jail.

In 1844 Joseph Smith campaigned for president to bring Mormon grievances to the nation's attention. There are no pictures of candidate Smith. This presidential campaign ad directed voters (in Latin) to build upon the rock of truth and vanquish error by electing Joseph Smith.

13. LINCOLN'S FAILED MURDER CASE

The second Hancock County Courthouse was new in 1839 when Lincoln represented William Fraim. The Fraim murder case was one of the first trials held in the building. Court and county offices were on the first floor; a well-lighted courtroom occupied the second floor. The courthouse was demolished to make room for the current courthouse, completed in 1908.

ABRAHAM LINCOLN LOST A MURDER CASE HERE IN APRIL 1839.

A drunken Irish deckhand, William Fraim, killed a shipmate while their steamboat was docked on the Illinois River in Schuyler County across from Beardstown. When the shipmate blew cigar smoke in his face, Fraim attempted to knock the cigar from the smoker's mouth. Meeting resistance, Fraim drew *"a long butcher knife from his side and drove it to the hilt"* in the victim's chest. Local citizens were outraged, and Fraim got his case moved to a supposedly more neutral setting in Hancock County. The young circuit-riding attorney Abraham Lincoln was assigned to defend him. The trial lasted one day, the jury finding Fraim guilty. Lincoln tried to set the judgment aside but failed. Three weeks later Fraim was hung—the only client that Lincoln lost to a hangman's noose. Among the jury members in this case was Daniel H. Wells, a prominent early Hancock County settler who later joined the Mormons and became Brigham Young's counselor in the Church presidency.

ILLINOIS JURIES USUALLY

acquitted defendants in murder trials in Lincoln's day—which made the Fraim case even more remarkable. (Lincoln's clients escaped execution in 25 of 26 murder cases where he was defense attorney.) The relative infrequency of public hangings made them memorable local events in frontier Illinois. The people of Carthage were typical of the time in their enthusiastic attendance. Officials constructed a special gallows in a kind of "natural amphitheater" in a field just southeast of town. School was dismissed for children to attend; many families treated the affair as a kind of picnic. Carthage did not experience another murder trial in its courthouse until six years later, when in May 1845 a local jury followed the usual pattern and acquitted all defendants accused of the murder of Joseph Smith.

James H. Ralston, the judge who presided over the Fraim trial, was a Democrat from Quincy who occasionally provided legal counsel to Joseph Smith.

Fraim trial jury member Daniel H. Wells was a prominent early Hancock County resident of Commerce (later Nauvoo), Illinois.

1858 Senate Campaign
in Hancock County

Ⓛ Lincoln Speech
Ⓓ Douglas Speech

Hancock County hosted none of the famous Lincoln-Douglas campaign debates of 1858. But Lincoln gave more formal speeches here (four) than in any other county during the 1858 senatorial campaign. Stephen Douglas spoke in Hancock County three times—more than in any other county except one (Madison).

ABRAHAM LINCOLN DEFENDED HIMSELF AGAINST POLITICAL

attacks during much of the speech he delivered here on the courthouse grounds on October 22, 1858. Stephen A. Douglas, who had spoken here 11 days earlier, accused Lincoln of being too cozy with big railroad companies and of helping them to avoid paying taxes—a charge Douglas had never made to Lincoln's face in their joint debates. Lincoln explained his fee arrangement for railroad legal services and pro-claimed that railroads *"shall not be released from their obligations to pay money into the State Treasury."* Despite the necessity of responding to attacks, Lincoln seemed to be *"in admirable spirits and voice and gave us the best speech ever made in Hancock County,"* reported Republican newspapers. Apparently there were many more women at Lincoln's speech than at Douglas's. The local Democratic newspaper excused this embarrassment by blaming a heavy rain the night before Douglas spoke that had turned Carthage into a sea of mud, and boasting that more "real" voters (men) had attended Douglas's speech.

Lincoln came to Carthage one week after the last of his famous joint debates with Douglas. He made a last-minute strategic decision to spend two days contesting Hancock County as the Senate race neared its frantic close. Lincoln had this picture taken 11 days before he spoke in Carthage.

ILLINOIS GOVERNOR THOMAS FORD

paraded Joseph and Hyrum Smith as prisoners before assembled militia troops on these courthouse grounds the morning after the Mormon leaders surrendered to answer riot charges. Some of the troops rebelled at the Mormon prisoners being introduced with military dignities, forcing the governor to intervene. Later that day the Smiths were released, pending trial in the autumn. But justice of the peace Robert F. Smith (also militia captain of the Carthage Greys) ordered the Smiths rearrested on new charges of treason. The courthouse was *"crowded to suffocation"* when the prisoners were escorted there through menacing crowds the next day—June 26, 1844. Their case was held over yet again, but the Smiths were murdered before they could return.

Fourteen years before Lincoln and Douglas spoke here, Joseph and Hyrum Smith were paraded before hostile militia troops on these same courthouse grounds.

15. LINCOLN'S AGRICULTURAL WORLD

The original Hancock County commissioner's court seal, adopted in 1833, featured a plow and a steamboat, which reflected dreams of the first white settlers for productive farms and expanding markets. The emergence of wheat as an important frontier market crop caused county residents to redesign the court seal in 1837 to feature a sheaf of wheat. Yet as late as 1835 early settlers were still feeding their horses grass cut from the open prairie where the courthouse now stands.

AGRICULTURAL LIFE HAS
defined the very essence of Hancock County from the earliest days of its Anglo-American settlement. Lincoln, however, seemed indifferent to agriculture. Once he left his father's home, Lincoln never farmed again. But he came to respect the enlightened practice of *"scientific"* husbandry that in his time came to characterize much of American agriculture. Lincoln urged *"deeper plowing, analysis of soils,*

experiments with manures, and varieties of seeds." He delighted in the ingeniousness of labor-saving farm implements and championed the *"application of steam power to farm work."* This attitude made him an important supporter of the agricultural land grant college system. Speaking before the Wisconsin State Agricultural Society he declared, *"[F]armers, being the most numerous class, it follows that their interest is the largest interest. It also follows that that interest is most worthy of all to be cherished and cultivated."*

"KEEP A STRICT OUTLOOK OVER

the prairies towards Nauvoo," the captain of the Carthage Greys ordered 14-year-old William R. Hamilton, son of the Hamilton House proprietor, as he scampered up to the courthouse cupola at midday on June 27, 1844. Earlier, Governor Thomas Ford had detailed the Greys to guard the Mormon leaders Joseph and Hyrum Smith incarcerated in the Carthage jail, two blocks to the northwest. The Greys were encamped on the southwest corner of the courthouse square—and were apparently unprepared several hours later when young Hamilton shouted that a body of armed men was approaching the jail. *"I have always thought the officers and some privates were working for delay,"* Hamilton stated years later. *"The company finally reached the jail, but not until after the mob had completed their work."*

As a boy, William Hamilton raised the alarm of armed men approaching the Carthage jail—a warning that received a tardy response from the guarding militia.

16. HAMILTON HOUSE

Hamilton House.

ABRAHAM LINCOLN PROBABLY STAYED AT THE HAMILTON HOUSE

when he came to Carthage in 1839 to represent the defendant in the Fraim murder trial. There are no other known Lincoln court cases in Hancock County. But he did handle several local cases on appeal in the Illinois State Supreme Court—including an 1845 case where the owner of the Hamilton House, Artois Hamilton, sued a debtor for payment. In *Moore v. Hamilton*, Lincoln persuaded the Supreme Court to throw out a jury verdict favoring Hamilton (though Hamilton ended up winning when the case was retried in Carthage the next year with different lawyers). Lincoln apparently didn't visit Carthage again until the 1858 Senate race against Stephen A. Douglas. Artois Hamilton most likely didn't vote for Lincoln in 1858—not because he was sore about an old court case but because he was a Democrat and his son, William R. Hamilton, ran for Hancock County sheriff that year on the Democratic ticket headed by Douglas. Both Douglas and young Hamilton won.

"THOSE ARE THE BOYS THAT WILL

settle you Mormons," Artois Hamilton
warned a Mormon acquaintance while
pointing at the Carthage Greys—who
were prominent among the local militia
units that excitedly pressed for a glimpse
of Joseph Smith when he arrived here
just before midnight on June 24, 1844.
Governor Thomas Ford was already quartered in Hamilton's—as were many of the
Prophet's apostate Mormon enemies. The
Mormon company spent the night and
most of the next day at Hamilton's until
they were imprisoned in the Carthage
jail on the evening of June 25. Two days
later, Hamilton brought the bodies of
Joseph and Hyrum Smith back to his inn
after they were murdered at the jail. He
prepared pine board boxes for the corpses
and helped transport them in wagons to
Nauvoo the next morning.

Secretary of State John Hay.

*Artois Hamilton established Carthage's
first inn, the Hamilton House, in 1835. He
ran it until 1851—the year his wife, two
children, and two sisters died in a cholera
epidemic. Many Lincoln-era dignitaries
stayed here, including Warsaw's John
Hay, who became a confidential secretary
to President Lincoln during the Civil
War and served as secretary of state
under presidents William McKinley and
Theodore Roosevelt. Hay also wrote a
famous account of the assassination of
Joseph Smith for* Atlantic Monthly.

Artois Hamilton.

17. LINCOLN'S "CONFIDENTIAL FRIEND"

Alexander Sympson, a Kentucky boyhood friend of Lincoln's, had this image taken in Tennessee while serving in the Union army during the Civil War. Lincoln stayed at the Alexander Sympson home (which once stood at the southwest corner of Cherry and Marion in Carthage) during his 1858 campaign visit. The Sympsons hosted many gala events, sometimes serving dinner to as many as 300 people at one sitting. Sympson's daughter recalled, "In those days when the unexpected visitor was the expected thing, I could catch, kill, dress and fry a chicken in thirty minutes."

ALEXANDER SYMPSON WAS THE most optimistic of local Lincoln enthusiasts during the 1858 Senate race. While others marveled, he felt vindicated at the thousands of people *"rained down from a cloudless sky"* to greet Lincoln in Carthage on October 22, 1858. Sympson hosted Lincoln in his home. The house became the focal point of a grand procession of wagons and carriages that streamed into Carthage from all directions. Multitudes marched by, cheering Lincoln in a parade stretching *"over three miles long"* that *"wound all around & through town & around the public square."* Not even the accidental explosion of a ceremonial cannon (the attending captain lost a finger and the rammer suffered burns on his face and arms) dampened the excitement. Sympson was on Lincoln's short list of *"confidential friends."* Lincoln trusted him with a delicate political task—to quietly encourage local supporters of President James Buchanan in his intraparty feud with Stephen Douglas in hopes of splitting the Democratic Party and weakening Douglas. The strategy failed.

SYMPSON KNEW LINCOLN WHEN THEY WERE SMALL BOYS IN

Kentucky. He remembered Lincoln as *"the shyest, most reticent, most uncouth and awkward-appearing, homeliest and worse dressed"* of all their peers. It was inevitable that such a child would suffer ridicule. According to Sympson, several larger boys attacked Lincoln as he stood by a tree. *"Lincoln soundly thrashed the first, second and third in succession, and then placed his back against the tree, defied the whole crowd and taunted them with cowardice. But he was disturbed no more."* Like Lincoln, Sympson moved to Illinois in the 1830s. He arrived in Carthage in early 1844 just as contention with the Mormons was peaking. Like most Whigs, he joined the anti-Mormon party. Fifteen years later he joined the Union army and died two years after Lincoln's assassination.

President Lincoln wrote this note during the Civil War requesting that a government position be found for the son of his old friend Alexander Sympson.

PART 3. GREATER HANCOCK COUNTY

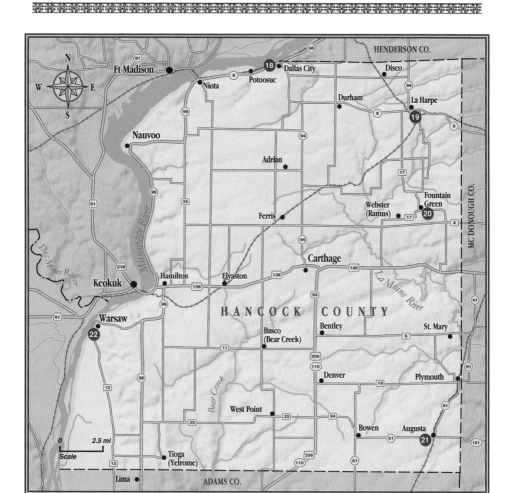

Map of Hancock County, Illinois, identifying story locations with corresponding story numbers.

18. LINCOLN COMES TO DALLAS CITY

Dallas City as it appeared in the Civil War era. Twenty years earlier, Nauvoo merchants John M. Finch and William H. Rollosson founded the community when they moved their store to this location, following the turmoil surrounding the murder of Joseph Smith in 1844 (neither man was a Mormon). Being staunch Democrats, they named their town after Democratic vice president George M. Dallas. Finch laid out the town in 1848. But it wasn't until Lincoln spoke here in 1858 that civic leaders were able to gather enough signatures from the crowd to petition for a city charter (which the state legislature granted in 1859).

LINCOLN CAMPAIGNED IN DALLAS CITY DURING THE 1858

Senate race, but his opponent Stephen Douglas did not. This left local Democrats with no outlet for their partisan zeal other than to cause mischief during the Republican candidate's visit. Democrats hoisted a flag over the stand where Lincoln was speaking that declared, *"Douglas Against the World."* Lincoln supposedly quipped, *"Well, Douglas may be against the world, but always let it be said that Lincoln was for the world, and all the people that live in it!"* Reportedly, a rival Democratic speaker attempted to drown out Lincoln by shouting from a makeshift platform placed over a barrel. But someone pulled out a plank and the noisy orator fell into the barrel. One young girl remembered years afterward seeing Lincoln's *"tall frame mounted on a lumber pile delivering his address, despite interruption and heckling."* After spending the afternoon in Dallas City, Lincoln departed for an evening appointment on the other side of the county.

IN MID-JULY 1846, VIGILANTES

from the river town of Appanoose surrounded and whipped eight Mormons who were harvesting crops east of Nauvoo. A Nauvoo posse arrested several of the vigilantes. This action triggered a series of reprisals that occurred in the region around Dallas City. "Regulators" from neighboring Pontoosuc captured four Mormons—including Brigham Young's brother Phineas—who were traveling to a mill in the area to obtain flour for the exodus west. Led by local resident Jesse Wimp, described as *"a large muscular backwoodsman,"* the Regulators imprisoned the men with another previously captured Mormon in a riverside warehouse. A large posse immediately left Nauvoo in search of the prisoners. Their abductors stayed one step ahead, hiding the prisoners at various locations throughout the area by day and moving by night. They went as far upriver as Shokokon in Henderson County. The prisoners endured this treatment for two weeks, finally being released in exchange for the release of the Appanoose vigilantes.

Lincoln addressed area residents from a lumber pile on the riverfront outside H. F. Black's Lumberyard.

Brigham Young's brother Phineas Young was held hostage by anti-Mormons several weeks prior to the expulsion of the Mormons in September 1846.

The King family residence at 108 South C Street was almost new when Abraham Lincoln stayed here after delivering a campaign speech in La Harpe's Methodist Church on the evening of October 23, 1858. The podium Lincoln used is in the current church built on the location of the original one at 102 North First Street. Other Lincoln-related artifacts are displayed in the La Harpe Historical Society Museum.

PEOPLE LINED THE STREETS WHEN ABRAHAM LINCOLN MADE

his 1858 campaign stop in La Harpe. But not everyone wished him well. Local Democrats tried to disrupt the activities—by, among other things, throwing bricks—but the wagon carrying the Republican senatorial candidate made it safely to the Methodist Church, where Lincoln addressed a capacity crowd. Lincoln's relatives from nearby Fountain Green undoubtedly attended the big event. Among them would have been 27-year-old Hezekiah Lincoln, a farmer and merchant who ran several stores and was reportedly La Harpe's first resident attorney. His brother Robert, who lived in Carthage, was the Republican candidate for Hancock County sheriff and was on the 1858 Republican ticket with his famous cousin. Neither of the Lincolns won their races that year.

UPON ARRIVING IN LA HARPE,

Lincoln reportedly visited with prominent Republicans in the Tuttle Hotel. Mr. Tuttle was one of La Harpe's founders and a wealthy man. The story is told that in the 1840s when county residents were trying to drive away the Mormons, a meeting was held in La Harpe to raise money for the effort. When asked if he would contribute he remained silent, later claiming that he was partially deaf and hadn't heard the request. But when asked in a similar meeting years later to contribute land to persuade railroad officials to run a line through La Harpe, Tuttle miraculously heard clearly and replied instantly that he would contribute (thereby increasing the value of his remaining lands and business). His reluctance to fund anti-Mormon activities may have partially been due to his acquaintance with several respected early La Harpe settlers who became Latter-day Saints, including merchant and mill operator Lewis Rice Chaffin (who helped select the town's name) and Dr. George Coulsen, who built what became La Harpe's first schoolhouse. Mormons established a church branch here in 1841, which was frequently visited by church leaders such as Apostles Brigham Young and John Taylor.

Hezekiah Lincoln—first cousin, once removed, of President Lincoln (son of Lincoln's first cousin Abraham Lincoln, of neighboring Fountain Green, Illinois).

Hezekiah Lincoln is buried in the La Harpe cemetery along with his wife, Phoebe, and his unmarried brother Nicholas.

Thomas Lincoln (son of the president's cousin James) and his wife, Emily, stand beside the banner won by Fountain Green's company of "Wide Awakes" for having the largest delegation at the Republican rally in Keokuk, Iowa, during Lincoln's 1860 presidential campaign. The banner now hangs in Springfield's Old State Capitol. Twelve of Lincoln's Hancock County relatives are buried in the old Catholic cemetery about 1.3 miles east of the Fountain Green village square.

FOUNTAIN GREEN'S ABRAHAM

Lincoln was the president's cousin. His father, Mordecai, was the oldest brother of the president's father. His mother, Elizabeth, was a devout Catholic. She raised Abraham and his five siblings in the faith. Like his father, Abraham also married an Elizabeth. In 1830 they joined the rest of the family in moving from Kentucky to this area. Mordecai froze to death in a blizzard shortly after arriving. But his sons Abraham and James became important early Fountain Green settlers. Their farms prospered. Both served as justices of the peace. They helped establish a Catholic church here. Though good-natured, the Lincolns were known for occasional melancholy. Abraham's daughter Mary Jane was judged insane later in life. His youngest brother Mordecai Jr. was considered eccentric and never married. Abraham died in 1852 and did not live to see his cousin elected president. Though his son Robert Lincoln lost in his run for Hancock County sheriff on the same 1860 Republican ticket headed by his famous relative, in Fountain Green Township Republicans won a small plurality.

COLONEL THOMAS GEDDES WAS A

political associate of the future president when Lincoln served in the Illinois state legislature. An old-line Whig leader, he later became Fountain Green's leading Republican. Geddes was a parade marshal when Lincoln spoke in Carthage during the 1858 senatorial contest against Stephen Douglas. Geddes received his military title a decade earlier when he served as a militia officer against the Mormons in June 1844, September 1845, and September 1846. By contrast, Fountain Green's Abraham Lincoln surveyed a local road in 1843 with his Mormon neighbor Charles Chrisman and appears not to have taken an active role in anti-Mormon activities. In fact, on the day that Joseph Smith was murdered, Lincoln performed the marriage of a neighbor couple in his role as justice of the peace. Perhaps being Catholic—another vilified religion in 19th-century America—tempered his attitude toward the Mormons.

Colonel Thomas Geddes—friend of Lincoln, foe of the Mormons.

There is no known photograph of the president's cousin Abraham Lincoln. His headstone lies in the old Catholic Cemetery near Fountain Green.

James Stark cast a vote for Lincoln in the Electoral College.

ELECTION, NEXT TUESDAY, NOV. 6.
" No Postponement on account of the Weather."

REPUBLICAN NOMINATIONS.

For President,

Abraham Lincoln.

For Vice President,

Hannibal Hamlin.

FOR PRESIDENTIAL ELECTORS.

ELECTORS AT LARGE:

LEONARD SWETT,   JOHN M. PALMER.

DISTRICT ELECTORS:

First District—ALLEN C. FULLER.
Second District—WILLIAM B. PLATO.
Third District—LAWRENCE WELDON.
Fourth District—WILLIAM P. KELLOGG.
Fifth District—JAMES STARK.
Sixth District—JAMES C. CONKLING.
Seventh District—H. P. H. BROMWELL.
Eighth District—THOMAS G. ALLEN.
Ninth District—JOHN OLNEY.

"ONE OF YOUR SLEDGE HAMMER *speeches will effect wonders,"* declared the man who invited Lincoln to attend the district convention held in Augusta on August 25, 1858. Putting aside concerns that it might be overcrowding his agenda for the Senate race against Stephen Douglas (their second debate was scheduled for two days later in Freeport), Lincoln came anyway. He arrived by train and spent the morning at the convention where local Republicans nominated his friend Jackson Grimshaw for Congress. In the afternoon he gave a campaign speech in John Catlin's Grove. Local organizers had promised Lincoln *"the tallest kind of a crowd"*—and he wasn't disappointed. Over 1,200 people stood listening in the rain. Reporters quipped that the crowd *"didn't come to hear a dry speaker, and he wasn't addressing a dry audience."* Republicans

During his 1858 visit to Augusta, Lincoln was a guest at the home of James Stark for a midday meal of "Irish and sweet potatoes, honey, green beans, and peach cobbler." Always the savvy politician, Lincoln reportedly declared he "could eat a gallon [of the beans] if they were cooked as good as Mrs. Stark cooked them." Two years later, as an Illinois presidential elector, Stark had dinner with the president-elect in Springfield after officially casting his electoral vote for Lincoln.

The Stark home.

anticipated winning in Augusta by a large majority. So when their majority turned out to be just three votes they suspected fraud. *"This damned town came very near fleeing to the camps of [the Democrats],"* complained one disgruntled Republican.

LINCOLN NEARLY FELL FROM THE

buggy that carried him through crowded Augusta during his 1858 campaign visit. The driver, John Catlin, reported that whenever Lincoln stood to acknowledge cheers he startled the horses, which were unaccustomed to such a tall passenger, causing them to jerk the buggy—forcing Lincoln to grab Catlin's shoulder for support to avoid tumbling out. Catlin continued to support Lincoln after war broke out several years later, serving as adjutant to the colonel commanding the Illinois 2nd Cavalry Regiment from Hancock County. As a younger man Catlin had seen militia service during the time of the Mormon troubles. On the night the Mormon leaders Joseph and Hyrum Smith were murdered at Carthage, Augusta became a city of refuge for frightened county residents who fled here fearing Mormon retaliation

Buggy driver John Catlin.

22. LINCOLN'S WARSAW SECRETARY

John Hay, pictured in his late teens, became one of President Lincoln's personal secretaries at the age of 22.

The Hay family home in Warsaw, Illinois.

THE SUPPORT OF WHIG

legislator Abraham Lincoln for internal improvements in the 1836–37 Illinois legislature aligned him with Warsaw's Whig legislator Mark Aldrich and other local land speculators (future Mormon foes) who pushed for new state roads and a Warsaw railroad to Peoria. Lincoln's future secretary, John Hay, imbibed Whig attitudes during his Warsaw youth. In his teens, Hay left town for educational advancement but returned frequently to be with family. Writing from wartime Washington, D.C., he wistfully described Warsaw as a *"as a social paradise compared with this miserable sprawling village."* But during a quick visit home at a low point during the Civil War he found *"Copperheads"* (antiwar dissidents) *"exultant"* and local citizens *"growling & despondent."* In 1880 he gave his *"first speech of any length in the open air"* in the square in front of his elderly father's Warsaw home while campaigning for James Garfield. Hay

"[T]he great river was the scene of my early dreams," John Hay wrote of his Warsaw childhood. As a young boy he lived in his physician father's comfortable home and attended grammar school in what he affectionately dubbed the "Little Brick Schoolhouse." "The boys of my day led an amphibious life," Hay remembered. "We built snow forts and called them the Alamo; we sang rude songs. . . . [and listened for] the loud puffing and whistling steamers of olden times."

Warsaw's "Little Brick Schoolhouse."

later served many diplomatic appointments for the United States, including secretary of state under presidents William McKinley and Theodore Roosevelt.

AS A CHILD, JOHN HAY WITNESSED

the deep anti-Mormon fervor that gripped the region during the 1840s. Warsaw—home of Thomas Sharp's incendiary newspaper, the *Warsaw Signal*—was the epicenter of the anti-Mormon crusade. At first, Whig land developers led by Mark Aldrich courted Mormon settlement on lands south of town. The developers lost heavily when Mormons abandoned the settlement because of exorbitant rent and commodity prices. Resentful Whigs like Aldrich and disgruntled former Democrats like Sharp and William E. Roosevelt (uncle of the future president Theodore Roosevelt) joined to oppose expanding Mormon economic and political power. Warsaw residents Aldrich, Sharp, Jacob C. Davis, and William N. Grover were tried for the murder of Joseph Smith and were acquitted. During the 1850s, former anti-Mormon allies split over the slavery issue. Some such as Sharp supported Lincoln; others such as Roosevelt supported Stephen Douglas.

Thomas Sharp, editor of the Warsaw Signal, *in his later years. He was in his early 20s when he became the chief editorial nemesis of the Mormons.*

PART 4. NAUVOO-TO-SPRINGFIELD TRAVEL ROUTE

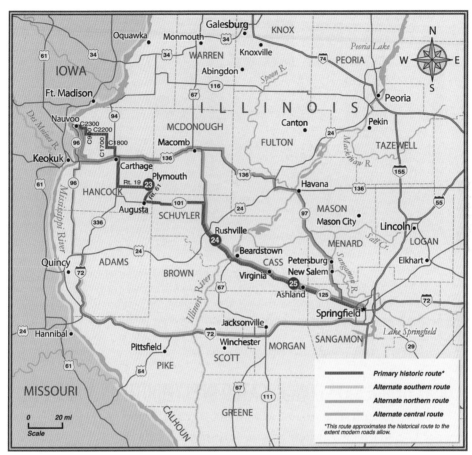

Joseph Smith made a cold wintertime trip from Nauvoo to Springfield to test the validity of a Missouri writ of extradition in Federal Court. He was gone from December 27, 1842, to January 10, 1843. The journey took four days and three nights each way. He stayed at the same inns both going and returning. The route and towns along the way were also familiar to Abraham Lincoln. Visitors may follow the map's primary route to approximate Joseph Smith's journey. Alternate routes between Nauvoo and Springfield provide travelers additional opportunities to explore Lincoln- and Mormon-related landscapes within the Abraham Lincoln National Heritage Area. Story locations are identified by corresponding numbers.

Story Site Locations
23. Lincoln-Era Plymouth
24. Lincoln's Rushville Reception
25. Captain Dutch's Halfway House

23. LINCOLN-ERA PLYMOUTH

This "lynch-pin" buggy constructed by George Chapman may have been Hancock County's first carriage when he brought it to the Plymouth area in the early 1830s. Local tradition holds that Chapman and his son-in-law, Thomas "Jeff" Holtsclaw, transported Lincoln in it from Plymouth to Carthage in the early morning of October 22, 1858, for the giant Republican rally there. The night before, Holtsclaw—a former Springfield neighbor of Lincoln's—reportedly hosted him at his home two miles northwest of town.

LOCAL DEMOCRATS CONGREGATED IN PLYMOUTH ON AUGUST 12,

1858, to nominate a state senator who would vote for Stephen A. Douglas for the U.S. Senate in the next legislative session. Douglas himself stopped to campaign here late on October 9—giving one of his shorter speeches (45 minutes). The town's entire population of 1,000 turned out as Douglas arrived on the train from Macomb. It's probable that the "Little Giant" rested here on Sunday, October 10—most likely at Plymouth's renowned hostelry, the Cuyler House—before departing on a muddy carriage ride to Carthage the next day. Lincoln came through several days later on October 21 on his way to Carthage. He delivered no formal speech in Plymouth. He departed in an old buggy owned by local Democrat George Chapman. On spying Chapman in the crowd at Carthage, Lincoln reportedly shouted for him to come forward, introduced him as his *"democratic friend"* and sat him among the Republican dignitaries on the stand. *"I hope you become a Republican before I leave,"* Lincoln quipped. It worked. Chapman turned Republican.

Today the "Lincoln Buggy" is on display in the Knox County Historical Museum in Knoxville, Illinois.

MORMON APOSTLE WILLIAM SMITH, A YOUNGER BROTHER OF JOSEPH

Smith, moved to Plymouth in 1839 and established a tavern inn that was just north of the town square. In 1842 he was elected with support by Mormons and non-Mormons alike on the Democratic ticket to the state legislature, where he observed Abraham Lincoln defend a Supreme Court justice from removal. Another Smith brother, Samuel, minded the Plymouth inn while William served in Springfield. Their married sister, Katharine Salisbury, also lived in Plymouth. On his way to and from Springfield for a court hearing in the winter of 1842–43, Joseph Smith stayed the night in Plymouth at his brother's inn, and enjoyed visits with Samuel and Katharine. On the return trip to Plymouth, the Prophet's party suffered a carriage accident, highlighting the dangers of 19th-century wintertime travel.

William Smith—state legislator and innkeeper. Courtesy Community of Christ.

Katherine Smith Salisbury—sister of Joseph and William Smith. Courtesy Community of Christ.

24. LINCOLN'S RUSHVILLE RECEPTION

The Schuyler County Courthouse in Lincoln's day occupied the center of the public square. During the 1858 Senate campaign, Lincoln spoke from a stand erected on the north side of the courthouse. As a lawyer he participated in 18 Schuyler County cases, mostly in the 1830s and 1840s. The Prophet Joseph Smith also knew this building, having stayed nearby twice at Mrs. Stephenson's Bell Tavern while traveling between Nauvoo and Springfield for a court hearing during the winter of 1842–43.

"BOYS, THIS IS A SHAKY *platform, but the Republican party has a strong foundation,"* exclaimed a tottering Abraham Lincoln perched atop a pedestal in the yard of his Rushville host, William Ray, on the evening of October 19, 1858. A tremendous procession of the region's excited Republicans had paraded through Rushville, terminating at the Ray residence, where they boisterously welcomed their champion against Stephen Douglas in the heated U.S. Senate contest. The next afternoon Lincoln gave a rousing speech outside the courthouse. The county's Democrats were also out in force. During the night someone hung a black flag from the courthouse spire. As Lincoln began, unruly boys on the rooftop raised a ruckus until the sheriff chased them away. From courthouse windows overlooking the scene, young female Douglas partisans heckled Lincoln until he finally rebuked them for their discourtesy. After the speech, Lincoln wrote a letter expressing fears that Democrats were importing Irish railroad workers from outside the county to illegally tip the scales in Douglas's favor. Republicans did indeed lose Schuyler County.

"WHY SCRIPPS, IT IS A GREAT PIECE OF FOLLY TO ATTEMPT TO MAKE

anything out of my early life," scoffed Abraham Lincoln when the influential Chicago newspaper editor John Locke Scripps asked him for information to write an 1860 presidential campaign biography. But Scripps persisted. Lincoln ultimately provided a brief autobiographical sketch which the editor used in writing a pamphlet titled *Life of Abraham Lincoln.* It became both an effective campaign document and an important historical source for students of Lincoln's life. The Scripps family was prominent in Rushville. John spent his childhood here. Other family members continued to play important local roles even after John left in 1847 to eventually become editor of the *Chicago Press & Tribune.* President Lincoln demonstrated his gratitude by appointing Scripps postmaster of Chicago.

John Locke Scripps, in the 1860s. Years earlier, as he was finishing his last term at McKendree College in Lebanon, Illinois, he received news of Joseph Smith's murder. Fearful of retaliation by vengeful Mormons, he hurriedly prepared to return home to help his family to safety. But stories of Mormon revenge were false. Scripps was able to stay and graduate several weeks later.

LIFE
OF
ABRAHAM LINCOLN.

CHAPTER I.
EARLY LIFE.

His Ancestors—His Grandfather Murdered by Indians—His Parents—An Only Child—Adverse Circumstances—
Western Schools Fifty Years Ago—Removal to Indiana—Work in the Forest—Letter-Writer for the Neighborhood
—The First Great Sorrow—Character of his Mother—Reading the Scriptures—Self-Educated—First Books—Interesting Incident of Boyhood—Early Western Preachers.

IT is not known at what period the ancestors of Abraham Lincoln came to America. The first account that has been obtained of them dates back about one hundred and fifty years, at which time they were living in Berks County, Pennsylvania, and were members of the Society of Friends. Whence or when they came to that region is not known.

About the middle of the last century, the great-grandfather of Abraham Lincoln removed from Berks County, Pennsylvania, to Rockingham County, Virginia. There Abraham Lincoln, the grandfather, and Thomas Lincoln, the father of the subject of this sketch, were born. Abraham, the grandfather, had four brothers—Isaac, Jacob, John, and Thomas—descendants of whom are now living in Virginia, North Carolina, Kentucky, Tennessee, and Missouri. Abraham removed to Kentucky about the year 1780, and four years thereafter, while engaged in opening a farm, he was surprised and killed by Indians; leaving a widow, three sons, and two daughters. The eldest son, Mordecai, remained in Kentucky until late in life, when he removed to Hancock County, Illinois, where he shortly afterward died, and where his descendants still live. The second son, Josiah, settled many years ago on Blue River, in Harrison County, Indiana. The eldest daughter, Mary, was married to Ralph Crume, and some of her descendants are now living in Breckenridge County, Kentucky. The second daughter, Nancy, was married to William Brumfield, and her descendants are supposed to be living in Kentucky.

Thomas, the youngest son, and father of the subject of this sketch, by the death of his father and the very narrow circumstances of his mother, was thrown upon his own resources while yet a child. Traveling from neighborhood to neighborhood, working wherever he could find employment, he grew up literally without education. He finally settled in Hardin County, where, in 1806, he was married to Nancy Hanks, whose family had also come from Virginia. The fruits of this union were a daughter and two sons. One of the latter died in infancy; the daughter died later in life, having been married, but leaving no issue. The sole survivor is the subject of this sketch.

Abraham Lincoln was born in Hardin County, Kentucky, February 12th, 1809. It would be difficult to conceive of more unpromising circumstances than those under which he was ushered into life. His parents were poor and uneducated. They were under the social ban which the presence of slavery always entails upon poverty. Their very limited means and the low grade of the neighboring schools, precluded the expectation of conferring upon their children the advantages of even a common English education. The present inhabitants of the Western States can have but a faint idea of the schools which fifty years ago constituted the only means of education accessible to the poorer classes. The teachers were, for the most part, ignorant, uncultivated men, rough of speech, uncouth in manners, and rarely competent to teach beyond the simplest rudiments of learning—"spelling, reading, writing," and sometimes a very little arithmetic. The books of study then in vogue, would not now be tolerated in schools of the lowest grade. The school-house, constructed of logs, floorless, windowless, and without inclosure, was in admirable harmony with teacher, text-books, and the mode of imparting instruction.

In his seventh year, Abraham was sent for short periods to two of these schools, and while attending them progressed so far as to learn to write. For this acquirement he manifested a great fondness. It was his custom to form letters, to write words and sen-

ENTERED according to Act of Congress, in the year 1860, by the CHICAGO PRESS AND TRIBUNE CO., in the Clerk's Office of the District Court for the Northern District of Illinois.

First page of Scripps's 1860 Lincoln campaign biography.

25. CAPTAIN DUTCH'S HALFWAY HOUSE

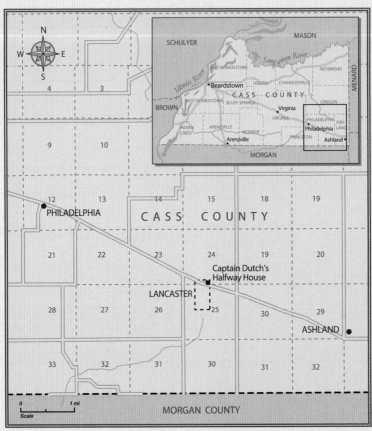

In May 1837, John Dutch, an affluent New England sea captain, laid out the town of Lancaster along the state road about halfway between Springfield and Beardstown. He constructed an elegant two-story tavern—the Halfway House—on the north side of the road where his family entertained overnight guests. The tavern prospered, but settlers failed to purchase lots in Dutch's open-prairie township. He abandoned Lancaster in June 1843. Today nothing remains of Dutch's Lancaster township.

CAPTAIN DUTCH HOSTED JOSEPH SMITH AND HIS ENTOURAGE

at the "Halfway House" tavern on the night of December 29, 1842, as the Prophet traveled to Springfield for an extradition hearing. *"[We had] much good music on the piano with singing in the evening,"* Joseph's diary records. This conformed to Illinois pioneer customs—as dancing and "charivaring"

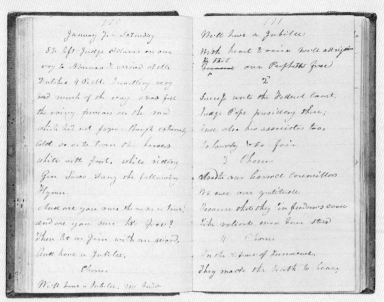

Lyrics in Joseph Smith's journal to a song sung at Captain Dutch's tavern celebrating the Mormon Prophet's court victory.

(mocking, boisterous serenading and noisemaking) was *"quite generally practiced as a means of amusement"* according to early local histories. Things were even more animated during their return trip on the night of January 7, 1843. Following a freezing day's ride from Springfield, the party thawed out at the tavern by composing and singing a jubilant ballad celebrating Joseph's court victory. *"The whole party were very cheerful and had a rich entertainment,"* Joseph's journal relates. Verses included praise for their host: *"And Captain Dutch we cannot pass without a word of praise, for he's the king of comic song as well as comic ways,"* and a tribute to the ladies of his family, *"who from soft piano bring such soul enchanting strains."*

IT IS NOT KNOWN IF ABRAHAM LINCOLN VISITED THE HALFWAY HOUSE,

but he was certainly familiar with the same route along which Joseph Smith's party traveled. About a year after the Prophet stayed with Captain Dutch's family, Lincoln spoke at Whig political meetings in the town of Virginia some few miles west of Lancaster. On Washington's Birthday in 1844 and again the next day, Lincoln declaimed *"the absurdities of locoism [the Democratic Party] and the soundness of Whig principles."* Democrats decried Lincoln's *"harangue"* as *"vulgar party vituperation."* In the other direction, about 3½ miles southeast of Lancaster, a cohort of Lincoln's fellow former Whigs (including Illinois' Civil War governor and Lincoln ally, Richard Yates) established the town of Ashland in 1857—named after the plantation home of Whig hero Henry Clay.

PART 5. SPRINGFIELD

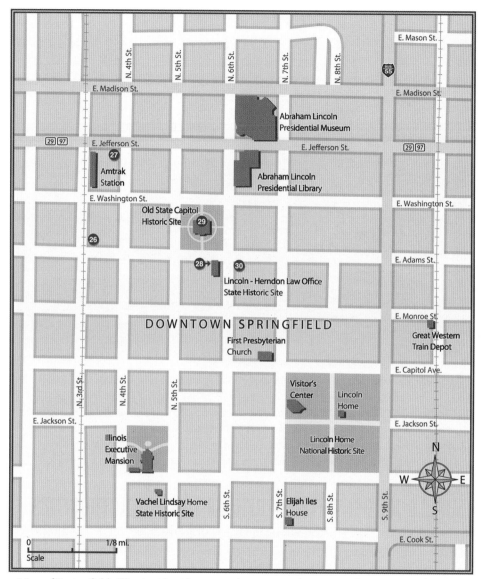

Map of Springfield, Illinois, identifying story locations with corresponding story numbers.

Story Site Locations
26. Globe Tavern
27. James Adams Residence
28. Federal Courtroom (Tinsley Building)
29. Old State Capitol
30. The American House

26. GLOBE TAVERN

The Globe Tavern as it appeared in 1865 at the time of Lincoln's funeral. Mormon leaders checked into the Globe Tavern when they arrived in Springfield on December 13, 1842, according to the journal of Apostle Willard Richards. Besides Richards and Hyrum Smith, other Mormons in attendance included Heber C. Kimball, William Clayton, and Reynolds Cahoon. They stayed for five days. Guests ate together. So it is possible that some of the Mormons may have shared a meal with tavern boarders Abraham and Mary Lincoln.

SHOULD JOSEPH SMITH SURRENDER TO STATE AUTHORITIES

in Springfield? That was the question that Mormon leaders made a winter trip to the state capital to discuss with leading lawyers and judges in December 1842. Missouri's governor wanted Illinois' governor to extradite Joseph Smith for allegedly conspiring to assassinate former Missouri governor Lilburn W. Boggs. The Prophet protested his innocence. U.S. district attorney Justin Butterfield had earlier written to the Prophet, urging him to come to Springfield to test his case. He and others believed that Missouri's demand would not stand up in court. So a delegation from Nauvoo led by Hyrum Smith and

Willard Richards made the cold December trip to Springfield. They discussed matters with Butterfield, Illinois secretary of state Lyman Trumbull, Illinois Supreme Court justice Stephen A. Douglas, and newly elected Illinois governor Thomas Ford (who also consulted with several supreme court justices). All concurred that Joseph should come to Springfield. This message the Mormon leaders took back to Nauvoo, arriving home a few days before Christmas 1842.

ABRAHAM AND MARY LINCOLN

were living here when Apostle Willard Richards and other Mormons lodged at the inn in December 1842. The Lincolns moved into the Globe upon their marriage on November 4, 1842. Mary's older sister Frances had previously lived in the same tavern during her first months of marriage to Dr. William Wallace. Still, becoming a boarder was a step down for Mary from the comfort and status she had enjoyed while living with her oldest sister, Elizabeth, wife of the politically and socially prominent Ninian Edwards. Mary gave birth to her first son, Robert, while she and her husband lived in the tavern. Boarders' complaints about Robert's crying and fussiness were reportedly a factor in their moving to a small rental cottage in the autumn of 1843.

Willard Richards was a Latter-day Saint apostle and a private secretary to Joseph Smith. He may have dined with the Lincolns at the Globe Tavern.

Joseph Smith slept on a couch in James Adams's parlor during his 1842–43 winter visit to Springfield. Adams was an early Springfield settler whose residence once stood on the southwest corner of Fourth and Jefferson Streets. A War of 1812 veteran and a New York militia general, Adams arrived in 1821 and became a lawyer and land speculator. He served in the Winnebago and Black Hawk Wars and ran unsuccessfully for governor in 1834. He later became the local probate judge.

"HE HAS BEEN A MOST

intimate friend," said Joseph Smith of Springfield's James Adams. Adams had first met Apostles Brigham Young and Heber C. Kimball when they stopped in Springfield in October 1839 on their way to serve missions in England. Joseph Smith passed through Springfield the next month, and noted, *"General James Adams, judge of probate, heard of me, sought me out, and took me home with him, and treated me like a father."* Adams was baptized a Latter-day Saint and eventually led the Church's Springfield branch. He also was the Prophet's political eyes and ears in the state capital. Later, he began dividing his time between Springfield and Nauvoo—where he became a regent of the University of Nauvoo and was ordained a Church Patriarch. He was among the first persons to participate in the temple endowment in the upstairs room of Joseph Smith's store. Adams had just been elected Hancock County probate judge when he suddenly died at Nauvoo on August 11, 1843, at the age of 60.

ABRAHAM LINCOLN DID NOT HAVE

a high opinion of James Adams. Adams was a prominent Democrat who helped young politicians such as Stephen Douglas early in their careers. In 1837 the general opposed Lincoln's good friend, Dr. Anson Henry, in the race for county probate judge. Lincoln attacked the general's integrity in a series of scathing newspaper articles known as the "Sampson's Ghost Letters." Adams handily won despite Lincoln's attacks. The future president learned from this episode to tone down his political rhetoric. Adams was also deputy grand master of Illinois Masons. He was a founder of Springfield's Masonic Lodge and supported the founding of the Nauvoo Masonic Lodge. Lincoln never became a Mason. Perhaps his distrust of Adams was a factor.

Springfield's first Masonic Hall.

The Nauvoo Masonic Hall as it appeared early in the 20th century.

28. FEDERAL COURTROOM (TINSLEY BUILDING)

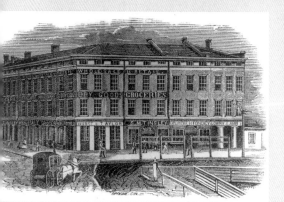

Seth Tinsley constructed this building in 1840 for his dry goods business. His store occupied the front section. He rented office space to lawyers on the second and third floors of the back section. The federal government also rented second-floor rooms in the back section for the U.S. District Court, judge's chambers, and a shared office for the court clerk, marshal, and others. It was here that Joseph Smith surrendered himself on December 31, 1842, to contest extradition to Missouri.

ALL OF SPRINGFIELD
society turned out to see Joseph Smith in federal court during the first week of January 1843. Spectators included an unusual number of women (reportedly including Mary Lincoln) eager to glimpse the celebrated Mormon prophet during his court hearing. Legal counsel had suggested that he file a habeas corpus petition to test the validity of Missouri's request. His attorneys were Justin Butterfield (a Chicago rival of Lincoln's in the Illinois Whig party) and Benjamin Edwards (brother-in-law of Mary Lincoln's sister, Elizabeth Edwards). Arguing for the government was Illinois attorney general Josiah Lamborn (who would later unsuccessfully prosecute the accused killers of Joseph Smith). As Smith and his party exited the court building onto Sixth Street following their first visit, a swearing crowd of detractors accosted them. U.S. marshal William Prentiss intervened to prevent violence. After

Justin Butterfield was a U.S. district attorney and the defense counsel for Joseph Smith.

three days of proceedings, federal district judge Nathaniel Pope ruled in the Prophet's favor.

LINCOLN KNEW WELL JUDGE

Nathaniel Pope and the federal courtroom in the Tinsley Building, being a frequent litigator there, particularly at the height of the 1842–43 bankruptcy stampede that followed passage of new federal bankruptcy laws. Lincoln and his senior partner Stephen T. Logan handled 72 bankruptcy cases in Pope's court. Perhaps Joseph Smith—whose bankruptcy petition Pope denied—would have done better had he employed Lincoln. It is possible that Lincoln witnessed a portion of Joseph's habeas corpus hearing, but there is no definitive evidence (he was defending an Illinois judge in a legislative hearing at the time). Several months later, Logan and Lincoln moved their office to the Tinsley Building. In 1844 Lincoln formed a new partnership with William Herndon, and they rented an office on the third floor. Today visitors can tour these rooms as part of the Lincoln-Herndon Law Office State Historic Site.

Benjamin Edwards, co-counsel for Joseph Smith, was a well-connected Whig lawyer who later switched parties to become a supporter of Democrat Stephen A. Douglas.

U.S. district judge Nathaniel Pope.

29. OLD STATE CAPITOL

When Mormons from the Zion's Camp expedition ventured through town on their way to Missouri in 1834, Springfield was not yet the state capital. No imposing capitol building filled the public square. The walls of the capitol were going up, however, when Joseph Smith stopped in Springfield in November 1839 on his way to Washington, D.C., to visit national leaders. The completed capitol building was the most prominent structure in Springfield when the Prophet came again in late December 1842, staying until early January 1843. Today it is open to visitors as a state historic site.

GRANTING THE NAUVOO CHARTER WAS ONE OF THE FIRST

actions state legislators took after they moved into their new chambers in the recently completed capitol building in December 1840. Two years later, when Joseph Smith arrived to contest extradition to Missouri, his presence in Springfield disrupted legislative proceedings. A team of runaway horses bolted past the capitol building, and someone yelled, *"Joe Smith is running away!"* This caused the House of Representatives to promptly adjourn in great consternation. Though invited to preach in the House chambers on New Year's Day, Joseph declined and remained in the audience as Elders Orson Hyde and John Taylor (Latter-day Saint apostles) spoke to a large assemblage that had hoped to hear the Mormon prophet. Joseph returned to the capitol during a recess in his court proceedings. He observed the Illinois State Senate. His journal records remarks critical of Senator Edward D. Baker, colonel of a state militia unit from Springfield, who had boasted of drilling his regiment to kill Joseph Smith or deliver him to the Missourians.

LINCOLN WAS IN THE CAPITOL'S HOUSE CHAMBER DEFENDING AN

Illinois Supreme Court justice in a removal hearing during the same week that Joseph Smith was fighting extradition in the federal courtroom across the street. The Prophet apparently observed none of the removal proceedings against Judge Thomas C. Browne. But his younger brother, William Smith (Hancock County's state representative), did. William Smith voted to sustain Lincoln's client, Judge Browne. It was in this same House chamber that Lincoln delivered his famous "House Divided" speech to kick off his 1858 senatorial contest against Stephen Douglas. Lincoln used the governor's office in the capitol for his headquarters during the 1860 presidential campaign and as president-elect. Finally, his body lay in state in the House chamber, visited by thousands of mourners, before burial in May 1865.

William Smith, brother of Joseph Smith, represented Hancock County in the state legislature.

Illinois Supreme Court judge Thomas C. Browne, whom Lincoln defended before the state legislature.

The American House was considered to be Springfield's fanciest hotel during the 1840s. Abraham Lincoln may have been among the crowd of 200 that patronized the place on its opening in November 1838. Its manager, a Bostonian named J. Clifton, promised "prompt and faithful" service and an unending supply of "every luxury that can be procured." The American House was a favorite place to entertain important visitors.

JOSEPH SMITH'S JOURNAL RECORDS TWO VISITS TO THE

American House. On December 31, 1842, he ate lunch there with his attorney, Justin Butterfield. On the same occasion he visited Governor Thomas Ford, who had a room there. Ford declared that he was not a *"religionist,"* but he discussed with Smith the Prophet's view of *"creeds,"* the Nauvoo temple, and the Nauvoo Legion. Ford expressed surprise that Joseph Smith had a normal appearance—that he was *"a very good looking man"*—for he had been led to believe that Mormons were a *"peculiar people . . . having horns or something of the kind."* Two days later Joseph Smith took lunch at the American House again, this time with Judge Nathaniel Pope and Judge Henry Brown. Brown, who was writing a history of Illinois, solicited information about the Mormons for his book. The Prophet obliged by providing several pamphlets and articles.

SPRINGFIELD ENJOYED "A SPLENDID BLOW OUT AND BALL AT THE

American Hotel on New Year's eve," wrote a New York newspaper reporter in January 1843. As was customary, newly elected U.S. senator Sidney Breese hosted a celebratory bash that far exceeded the expectations of the jaundiced New Yorker. Assuring easterners that Illinois ladies *"compare with any in the world,"* he wrote flatteringly about several women in attendance, including Mary Lincoln—whom he considered *"young, lively, and good looking."* Joseph Smith was in town for an extradition hearing. Did he meet the Lincolns at the New Year's Eve gala? Nothing in surviving historical sources indicates that he attended the festivities, though novelists have imagined otherwise.

A newspaper account of an American House political gala in December 1842 reported the "lively" appearance of newly married Mary Lincoln. This photograph of Mary—the earliest known—was taken four years later.

PART 6. ZION'S CAMP ROUTES

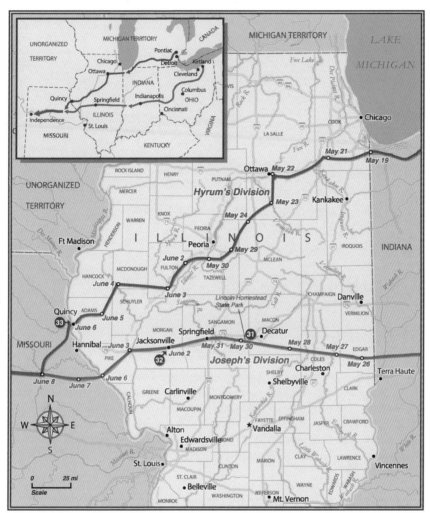

In May 1834, a relief expedition of about 200 armed Latter-day Saints from Ohio and other areas traveled to western Missouri in hopes of restoring displaced Mormon settlers who had been driven from their homes by mobs the previous winter. Joseph Smith led the largest contingent. His route traversed what today is the heart of Illinois' Abraham Lincoln National Heritage Area. His brother, Hyrum Smith, led a smaller contingent that also traveled across a portion of the National Heritage Area. The Mormons ultimately abandoned their effort when Missouri's governor refused to order state militia to assist them. Though the expedition—which came to be known as "Zion's Camp"—failed in its stated purpose, it proved to be an invaluable learning experience for future church leaders. Story locations are identified by corresponding numbers.

Story Site Locations

31. Macon County: First Home and Sham Battle

32. Jacksonville: Politics and Preaching

33. Quincy: Debate Site and City of Refuge

31. MACON COUNTY: FIRST HOME AND SHAM BATTLE

Lincoln's first Illinois home was a log cabin in rural Macon County. The cabin, pictured here in a 19th-century drawing, no longer exists. Today, a stone monument at the Lincoln Trail Homestead State Park marks the site. The marker overlooks the Sangamon River down which Lincoln paddled a canoe in 1831 when he left his family to strike out on his own. His parents moved that same year. Had they stayed, they most likely would have met Mormons from Zion's Camp who camped near their old homestead three years later.

DECATUR WAS A MUDDY FOREST CLEARING WITH A FEW

scattered cabins when 21-year-old Abraham Lincoln first passed through in March 1830. His family was looking for cousin John Hanks, who had moved to Illinois two years earlier. Hanks directed them to a spot on the north bank of the Sangamon River about ten miles west of town. There Lincoln helped his father build a cabin, clear land, and split rails. After an unusually long and cold winter—long remembered as *"the winter of the deep snow"*—Lincoln's parents moved again, backtracking to Coles County, Illinois. Lincoln did not follow. Instead he moved farther west, to the tiny Sangamon River village of New Salem. However, law and politics brought him back to Decatur frequently over the years. In Decatur at the 1860 Illinois Republican state convention, delegates nominated Lincoln for the presidency and kicked off the "Rail-splitter" campaign that resulted in Lincoln's nomination at the national convention in Chicago a few months later.

IT TOOK ZION'S CAMP FOUR WEEKS

to reach the spot west of Decatur where the Lincolns had originally homesteaded. As a diversion from hardships, Joseph Smith divided the camp into three parts and held a sham battle. Some attacked and some defended the main camp. *"Everything passed off with good feelings,"* one participant recorded, except that Captain Heber C. Kimball *"in receiving a charge, grasped [another captain's] sword blade and endeavored to take it from him,"* cutting the skin from the palm of his hand in the process. Later that day, Joseph Smith rebuked the camp cook for giving him sweet bread and the rest of the camp sour bread. The camp's youngest soldier, 16-year-old George A. Smith, recorded that the camp's leader *"wanted his brothers to fare as well as he did, and preferred to eat his portion of sour bread with them."*

Heber C. Kimball was 32 years old when he participated in Zion's Camp, and suffered a sword-cut hand during a training exercise. This image reflects the experience and maturity of later years when he served as a counselor to Church president Brigham Young.

32. JACKSONVILLE: POLITICS AND PREACHING

JOSEPH DUNCAN ASSUMED

the governor's chair at the same time Abraham Lincoln began his first term in the Illinois legislature. Duncan proposed a large internal improvements program for building roads, canals, and railroads that Lincoln passionately supported. Unfortunately, the program proved a financial disaster that brought the state to the brink of bankruptcy. Lincoln campaigned with Duncan in the state's southern counties, stumping for William Henry Harrison and other Whig candidates in the watershed election of 1840. But Illinois remained a Democratic stronghold, voting for Martin Van Buren. As the gubernatorial candidate for the minority Whig party in 1842, Duncan tried to attract voters beyond his party by attacking

Joseph Duncan, a four-term Democratic congressman from Jacksonville, Illinois, won the Illinois governorship in 1834. But he strayed from the Democrats, running again in 1842 by appealing to anti-Mormon sentiment as a Whig. He lost to Democrat Thomas Ford.

Joseph Duncan built this mansion in Jacksonville in 1834 at the beginning of his four-year term as governor. Because Illinois had no official residence for governors at the time, Duncan's home served as the state's executive mansion. Duncan reportedly sometimes teased his petite wife by lifting her high onto the parlor mantel. She couldn't get down without a servant's help. Whig legislator Abraham Lincoln likely visited the mansion. It has been restored by the Reverend James Caldwell Chapter of the National Society Daughters of the American Revolution and is open to visitors.

the Mormon theocracy in Nauvoo. Joseph Smith responded by naming his new horse "Jo Duncan"—taking amusement in symbolically riding the saddled and bridled animal wherever he wished.

RESIDENTS OF JACKSONVILLE MAY HAVE BEEN STARTLED ON THE

morning of Sunday, June 1, 1834, to hear the sound of a French horn blowing from the Mormon encampment on the outskirts of town. It was an invitation for all interested to come to Zion's Camp to hear Sabbath day preaching. Some 200 to 300 people assembled in the shade of a grove of trees where camp members climbed atop a large chest to address them. The men spoke on a variety of topics assigned to them by the Mormon Prophet. Speakers included Orson Pratt, Orson Hyde, and Brigham Young. Three years earlier (1831), the Prophet's brother, Hyrum Smith, had preached to a large crowd in the courthouse in Jacksonville during a mission trip through the area.

Sometime before the Saints were driven from Nauvoo, Mormon artist William W. Major painted this oil portrait of Joseph Smith addressing church leaders. All the men depicted (except for Willard Richards at the desk) participated in Zion's Camp—(left to right) Hyrum Smith, Richards, Joseph Smith, Orson Pratt, Parley P. Pratt, Orson Hyde, Heber C. Kimball, and Brigham Young. All eventually became members of the Church's Quorum of the Twelve Apostles that was organized the next year (1835), except for Hyrum, who later served as Church Patriarch and counselor to his brother.

33. QUINCY: DEBATE SITE AND CITY OF REFUGE

This bronze relief of Quincy's Lincoln-Douglas debate was the last completed work of the renowned sculptor Lorado Taft. Unveiled on the 78th anniversary of the debate in 1936, it remained at the center of debate site renovations completed in 2008 to commemorate the 150th anniversary of the Lincoln-Douglas Debates.

IN 1858 ABRAHAM LINCOLN

challenged incumbent Stephen A. Douglas for a seat in the U.S. Senate. As the country approached civil war, Americans confronted a dilemma: Can democracy resolve moral conflict? In a series of face-to-face debates held in seven Illinois cities, Lincoln and Douglas clashed over slavery, equality, and morality. Douglas held that morals are a matter of personal conscience and not a matter for political debate—*"It is for [slaveholders] to decide . . . the moral and religious right of the slavery question for themselves."* Lincoln held that there are moral absolutes and that personal opinion cannot turn something that is morally wrong into something that is right—*"[Douglas] cannot say people have a right to do wrong."* On October 13, 1858, the two men held their sixth debate on a wood platform under a towering linden tree in Washington Park in the center of Quincy. Twelve thousand people witnessed the spectacle. At the Quincy debate, Lincoln seemed to be gaining strength while Douglas seemed to be wearing down under the strain of the long campaign.

ALMOST TWENTY YEARS BEFORE

Lincoln and Douglas debated in Quincy's Washington Park, Mormon refugees fleeing a Missouri extermination order gathered on the park grounds in desperation during the winter of 1838–39. Quincy residents had pity on the homeless Mormons and took them in. This act of kindness burnished Quincy's reputation as an oasis of gentility and enlightened sentiment among the rough frontier river towns. Grateful Latter-day Saints considered Quincy a *"city of refuge"* as they regrouped before leaving to start a new settlement sixty miles upriver at Commerce, Illinois (later Nauvoo).

Governor Thomas Carlin entertained Joseph Smith and his wife, Emma, in his Quincy home on June 4, 1841—but waited until they left town to have Missouri extradition papers served on the Mormon Prophet. Judge Stephen A. Douglas ruled a few days later that the Missouri extradition writ was invalid and released Joseph Smith after a court hearing at Monmouth, Illinois.

Hyrum Smith, brother of Joseph Smith, led a contingent of Zion's Camp through Quincy on June 5, 1834. They purchased lead and ammunition before crossing the Mississippi River to join the main body of Zion's Camp in eastern Missouri.

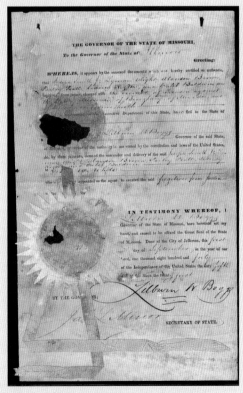

FOR FURTHER READING

ILLUSTRATION CREDITS

INDEX

FOR FURTHER READING

Bushman, Richard Lyman. "Joseph Smith and Abraham Lincoln." In *Joseph Smith and the Doctrinal Restoration*, 89–108. Provo, Utah: Brigham Young University Religious Center, 2005.

Hubbard, George U. "Abraham Lincoln as Seen by the Mormons." *Utah Historical Quarterly* 31, no. 2 (Spring 1963): 91–108.

Leonard, Glen M. *Nauvoo: A Place of Peace, a People of Promise.* Salt Lake City: Deseret Book and Brigham Young University Press, 2002.

Long, E. B. *The Saints and the Union: Utah Territory during the Civil War.* Urbana: University of Illinois Press, 1981.

Miller, Richard Lawrence. *Lincoln and His World: Prairie Politician, 1834–1842.* Mechanicsburg, Penn.: Stackpole Books, 2008.

———. *Lincoln and His World.* Vol. 3, *The Rise to National Prominence, 1843–1853.* Jefferson, N.C: McFarland, 2011.

Woodger, Mary Jane. "Abraham Lincoln and the Mormons." In *Civil War Saints*, edited by Kenneth L. Alford, 58–81. Provo, Utah: Brigham Young University Religious Studies Center; Salt Lake City: Deseret Book, 2012.

ILLUSTRATION CREDITS

All maps were created by Tom Willcockson of Mapcraft Cartography specifically for this book, except for the map of Nauvoo on page 24. All other images are courtesy of the Abraham Lincoln Presidential Library and Museum, Springfield, Illinois (a division of the Illinois Historic Preservation Agency), except for the following:

Institutional Repositories

- Brigham Young University Museum of Art, Provo, Utah (All rights reserved). p. 32—C. C. A. Christensen (1831–1912), *The Battle of Nauvoo*, ca. 1878, tempera on muslin, 76½ × 113½ inches, gift of the grandchildren of C. C. A. Christensen, 1970; p. 38—C. C. A. Christensen (1831–1912), *Joseph Mustering the Nauvoo Legion*, ca. 1878, tempera on muslin, 78 × 114 inches, gift of the grandchildren of C. C. A. Christensen. 1970.
- Community of Christ Archives, Independence, Missouri. Courtesy of Community of Christ Archives, World Headquarters, Independence, Missouri. p. 1—Joseph Smith; p. 35—Emma Smith with infant David Hyrum Smith; p. 40—Joseph Smith III; p. 41—Joseph Smith Mansion House; p. 75—William Smith; p. 75—Katherine Smith Salisbury.
- csdubya media. p. 75—image of Holtsclaw buggy (Lincoln buggy) at Knox County Historical Museum.
- Illinois State Military Museum, Department of Military Affairs, Springfield, Illinois. Courtesy of the Illinois National Guard and Militia Historical Society, Springfield, Illinois. p. 29—State militiamen; p. 45—Lincoln shooting at a wooden target; p. 45—Lincoln target.
- Knox County Historical Museum and Knox County Historical Sites, Inc., Knoxville, Illinois. p. 74—black-and-white image of Holtsclaw buggy (Lincoln buggy).
- LDS Church History Library, Salt Lake City, Utah. p. 30— *Expositor* office building; p. 35—Bernhisel note; p. 37— Daniel Wells's Nauvoo farmhouse; p. 37—Heber J. Grant;

p. 44—Jonathan Browning and wife; p. 51—Daniel H. Wells; p. 79—"Jubilee" Poem diary entry (image © by Intellectual Reserve, Inc.); p. 85—Nauvoo Masonic Hall; p. 89—William Smith; p. 99—Hyrum Smith.

- LDS Church History Museum, Salt Lake City, Utah © by Intellectual Reserve, Inc. p. 43—Joseph Smith death mask; p. 45—Browning's slide gun; p. 97—William Major (1804–54), *In Nauvoo 1843–1844 (Joseph Smith and His Friends)*, ca. 1844, oil on canvas, 23½ × 31½ inches.
- Library of Congress, Washington, D.C. p. 28—Edward D. Baker; p. 54—Oxen plow; p. 54—Steamboat; p. 94—Lincoln homestead near Decatur, Illinois; p. 96—Joseph Duncan House.
- Schuyler County (Illinois) Clerk. p. 76—Schuyler County Courthouse.
- Nicky Stratton. Springfield, Illinois. p. 67—Lincoln headstone.
- Utah State Historical Society, Salt Lake City, Utah. p. 36—Daniel H. Wells; p. 42—George Q. Cannon; p. 63—Phineas Young.

Public Domain Publications

- Gregg, Thomas. *History of Hancock County, Illinois, Together with an Outline History of the State, and a Digest of State Laws.* Chicago: Chas. C. Chapman, 1880. p. 57—Artois Hamilton; p. 68—James Stark.
- *An Illustrated Historical Atlas of Hancock County, Illinois: Map Work of Townships and Plats Made by Gen. Chas. A. Gilchrist.* Chicago: A. T. Andreas, 1874. p. 63—H. F. Black Lumber Company.
- Martha Board Chapter of the Daughters of the American Revolution, compilers, *Augusta's Story.* Augusta, Ill.: Augusta Eagle, 1921. p. 69—James Stark residence.
- *Portrait and Biographical Record of Hancock, McDonough, and Henderson Counties, Illinois.* Chicago: Lake City Publishing, 1894. p. 67—Thomas Geddes; p. 69—John Catlin.
- *The Prophet* (New York) 1, no. 6 (June 22, 1844), p. 2, col. 1. p. 49—Joseph Smith presidential campaign advertisement.

- Thayer, William Roscoe. *The Life and Letters of John Hay*, vol. 1. Boston: Houghton Mifflin, 1908. p. 70—Dr. Hay Home; p. 71—Little Brick Schoolhouse.
- Whitney, Orson R. *History of Utah: Comprising Preliminary Chapters on the Previous History of Her Founders, Accounts of Early Spanish and American Explorations in the Rocky Mountain Region, the Advent of the Mormon Pioneers, the Establishment and Dissolution of the Provisional Government of the State of Deseret, and the Subsequent Creation and Development of the Territory.* Salt Lake City, Utah: George Q. Cannon and Sons, 1892. p. 34—John M. Bernhisel; p. 83—Willard Richards; p. 95—Heber C. Kimball.

INDEX

***

at Springfield, 6; interrupted by runaway horses thought to be Joseph Smith escaping, 11, 88–89; Lincoln a member of, 24–25; Nauvoo charter passed by, 6, 88; William Smith a member of, 9, 75, 89

Illinois 2nd Cavalry Regiment, 69

Illinois State Bar Association, 13

Illinois State Capitol building (Springfield, 1840–76), 1, 5, 9, 12, 27, 66, 88–89; construction begins on, 4; construction completed on, 6, 88; House of Representatives meets for first time in, 6, 88; Joseph Smith observes legislature in, 89; Lincoln delivers "House Divided" speech in, 89; Lincoln has campaign headquarters in, 89; Lincoln's body lies in state in, 89; Mormons preach in, 12, 89; open as state historic site, 88

Illinois State Military Museum (Springfield), 45

Illinois State Supreme Court, 56

internal improvements, 70, 96

Jackson, "Stonewall," 42

Jacksonville (Illinois), 96–97

Jonas, Abraham, 30–31

Joseph Duncan Mansion House (Jacksonville), 96

Joseph Smith Mansion House (Nauvoo), 34, 40–41

Keokuk (Iowa), 66

Kibbe Hancock Heritage Museum (Carthage), 49

Kimball, Heber C., 4, 5, 82, 84, 97; suffers sword cut during military training with Zion's Camp near Decatur (Illinois), 95

King family (La Harpe), 64

Kirtland (Ohio), 3

Kirtland Camp, 4

Know-Nothings, 31

Knox County Historical Museum (Knoxville), 75

La Harpe (Illinois), 64–65

La Harpe Historical Society Museum, 64

Lamborn, Josiah, 10, 12, 14, 86

Lancaster (Illinois), 78–79

Law, Wilson, 11

Lebanon (Illinois), 77

Life of Abraham Lincoln (Scripps's campaign biography), 77

Lincoln, Abraham (president's first cousin), 17–18n15, 66–67

Lincoln, Abraham (U.S. president), 1; Abraham Jonas and, 30–31; agriculture and, 54–55; Alexander Sympson and, 58–59; American House opening possibly attended by, 90; assassination of, 29, 59; Augusta, campaigns in, 68–69; bankruptcy legal practice of, 87; body of, lies in state in Illinois State Capitol building, 89; Brigham Young and the Mormons treated by, like a tree stump to be plowed around, 15; burial of, 89; Carthage, campaigns in, 40, 52–53, 58; Dallas City, campaigns in, 62; Daniel Wells and, 36–37; defeated for U.S. Senate by Lyman Trumbull, 9; defends Illinois Supreme Court justice Thomas C. Browne in legislative removal hearing, 14, 75, 89; earliest-known photograph of, 25; 1858 U.S. Senate campaign and, 48, 52–53, 56, 58, 62, 64–65, 67, 68–69, 74, 76, 89; 1860 presidential campaign and, 66, 89; Edward D. Baker and, 28–29; engagement to Mary Todd, broken by, 6, 29; fights to protect himself during Kentucky childhood, 59; George Q. Cannon and, 42; Globe Tavern, resides at, 9, 82–83; Hamilton House, stays in, 56; helps father build cabin in Macon County, 94; "House Divided" speech delivered by, 89; House of Representatives, climbs out the window of, 6, 18n21; Illinois House of Representatives, serves in, 24–25; Illinois state militia, serves in, 29; internal improvements supported by, 96; James Adams and, 85; James Adams attacked in newspapers by, 7, 85; James W. Singleton and, 33; John C. Bennett's attacks on Mormons, response to, 8; John

Offutt, Denton, 2
Old State Capitol State Historic Site. *See*
Illinois State Capitol building
(Springfield, 1840–76)

Palmer, Abraham, 7
Palmer, Jonathan, 7
Peoria (Illinois), 70
Petersburg (Illinois), 2
Plymouth (Illinois), 74–75
Polk, James K., 15
Pontoosuc (Illinois), 63
Pope, Cynthia, 21n56
Pope, Lucretia, 21n56
Pope, Nathaniel, 10, 11, 12, 13, 14, 15, 87, 91;
rules in favor of Joseph Smith at federal
hearing in Springfield, 12, 87, 90–91
Pope, William, 14, 15
Pratt, Harry, 11
Pratt, Orson, 2, 97
Pratt, Parley P., 2, 97
Prentiss, William, 12, 14, 86

quarter (coin), commemorative U.S.
statehood series, 1–2
Quincy (Illinois), 12, 26, 27, 31, 44, 51; Lincoln-
Douglas debate held in, 98–99; Mormon
refugees from Missouri arrive at, 4, 99
Quorum of the Twelve Apostles, 97

Ralston, James H., 5, 9, 25, 51
Ray, William, 76
Remini, Robert, 15
Reorganized Church of Jesus Christ of Latter
Day Saints, 41
Republicans (political party), 27, 64, 66–67,
68–69, 76
Reynolds, Thomas, 10
Richards, Willard, 9, 82–83, 97
rifles (slide and repeating), 45
Rochester (Illinois), 4
Rockwell, Orrin Porter, 9
Rollosson, William H., 62
Roosevelt, Theodore, 57, 71
Roosevelt, William E., 71
Rushville (Illinois), 76–77

Salisbury, Katherine Smith, 75
Salt Lake City (Utah), 35
Sampson's Ghost Letters, 7, 19n29, 19n32, 85
Sangamo Journal (Springfield), 3, 8
Sangamon River, 94
Schuyler County Courthouse (Rushville), 76
Scripps, John Locke, 77
Sharp, Thomas, 71
Shawneetown (Illinois), 8
Shokokon (Illinois), 63
Singleton, James W., 32–33
Smith, David Hyrum, 35
Smith, Emma, 34–35, 99
Smith, George A., 95
Smith, Hyrum, 7, 9, 11, 15, 28, 33, 40, 43, 53,
55, 57, 69, 82; preaches at Jacksonville, 97;
preaches at Quincy, 99; Zion's Camp and,
93, 97, 99
Smith, Joseph, Jr., 1; bicentennial
commemoration for, 1; body of, brought
to Hamilton House, 57; campaigns for
U.S. presidency, 49; Captain Dutch's
Halfway House, stays at, 78–79; carriage
accident, suffers, 75; death mask of,
43; extradition attempts against, 9, 10,
11, 73, 82–83 86–87, 88–89, 99; federal
court hearing in Springfield attended
by, 10–14, 86–87; Hamilton House,
stays at, 57; horse named "Jo Duncan"
by, 97; James Adams's residence, stays
at, 84; murder of, 15, 28, 30, 33, 40, 41,
43, 49, 51, 53, 55, 57, 62, 67, 69, 71, 77;
Nathaniel Pope and Henry Brown met
by, at the American House, 91; New Year's
Eve party at American House, allegedly
attends, 11–12, 20n50; paraded before
militia troops on Carthage courthouse
square, 53; passes through Springfield
on way to Washington, D.C., 5, 84,
88; plural marriage introduced by, 8;
Plymouth, stays at, 75; Rushville, stays
at, 76; sermons delivered by Orson Hyde
and John Taylor in the state capitol
building attended by, 12; stakes outside
of Hancock County area dissolved by, 8;
Stephen A. Douglas and, 38–39; Thomas

Yates, Richard, 79

Young, Brigham, 5, 12, 26, 36, 51, 63, 84, 95; agrees that Mormons will leave Illinois beginning in spring 1846, 29; Jacksonville, preaches in, 97; John M. Bernhisel and, 34; Lincoln treats like a tree stump to be plowed around, 15; stays in Springfield while traveling to British mission, 4; visits church branch at La Harpe, 65

Young, Phineas, 63

Zion (Missouri), 3

Zion's Camp, 3, 88, 94–95, 97, 99; map of routes, 93

BRYON C. ANDREASEN is a historian at the LDS Church History Museum in Salt Lake City, Utah. Previously he was a research historian at the Abraham Lincoln Presidential Library and Museum in Springfield, Illinois, where he curated exhibits and conducted seminars and other public programming. The author helped create the Looking for Lincoln Heritage Coalition, a 501(c)3 corporation that pioneered heritage tourism in Illinois, and he authored the feasibility study on which Congress based legislation creating the Abraham Lincoln National Heritage Area. For ten years he was the editor of the *Journal of the Abraham Lincoln Association*—the premier scholarly journal in the field of Lincoln studies.

LOOKING FOR LINCOLN HERITAGE COALITION

BOARD OF DIRECTORS
Guy Fraker, Chair
Robert Davis
Richard Lynch
Laura Marks
Matthew Mittelstaedt
Daniel Noll
Dale Phillips
Joan Walters

STAFF
Sarah Watson, Executive Director
Jeanette Cowden
Heather Wickens

BOOK COMMITTEE
Bryon Andreasen
Dana Homann
Matthew Mittelstaedt
Kim Rosendahl
Sylvia Frank Rodrigue
Tim Townsend
Samuel Wheeler